1976
THE BRADFORD BOOK OF COLLECTOR'S PLATES

THE BRADFORD BOOK OF COLLECTOR'S PLATES
1976

McGRAW-HILL BOOK COMPANY
New York   St. Louis   San Francisco   Auckland   Dusseldorf   Johannesburg
Kuala Lumpur   London   Mexico   Montreal   New Delhi   Panama   Paris   Sao Paulo
Singapore   Sydney   Tokyo   Toronto

EDITED UNDER THE DIRECTION OF:
NADJA K. BARTELS
JOHN G. McKINVEN

THE OFFICIAL GUIDE TO ALL EDITIONS
TRADED ON THE WORLD'S LARGEST EXCHANGE

THE BRADFORD EXCHANGE
CHICAGO, ILLINOIS 60648

Library of Congress Cataloging in Publication Data

Bradford Exchange.
  The Bradford book of collector's plates.

  Includes indexes.
  1. Plates (Tableware)—Collectors and collecting.
  2. Plates (Tableware)—Catalogs. I. Bartels, Nadja K.
II. McKinven, John G. III. Title.
NK8596.B72   1976   738   76-16129
ISBN 0-07-007057-1
      0-07-007056-3   pbk.

Copyright © 1976 by McGraw-Hill, Inc. All rights reserved.
Printed in the United States of America. No part of this
publication may be reproduced, stored in a retrieval system,
or transmitted, in any form or by any means, electronic,
mechanical, photocopying, recording, or otherwise, without
the prior written permission of the publisher.

1234567890   DODO   785432109876

TABLE OF CONTENTS

INTRODUCTION
THE ARRANGEMENT OF
  THE LISTINGS I-6
THE BRADEX NUMBERS I-6
THE WORLD'S
  MOST TRADED ART I-7

DIRECTORY OF PLATES

4 ARGENTINA
Porcelana Granada 4-61-0.0

14 DENMARK
Bing & Grondahl 14-8-0.0
Georg Jensen 14-38-0.0
Svend Jensen 14-40-0.0
Royal Copenhagen 14-60-0.0

18 FRANCE
Cristal D'Albret 18-12-0.0
D'Arceau-Limoges 18-15-0.0
Haviland 18-30-0.0
Haviland Parlon 18-32-0.0
Lalique 18-46-0.0
Royal Limoges 18-69-0.0

22 GERMANY
Bareuther 22-6-0.0
Berlin 22-8-0.0
Danish Church 22-13-0.0
Dresden 22-15-0.0
Furstenberg 22-23-0.0
Goebel 22-27-0.0
Kaiser 22-42-0.0
Lihs Lindner 22-47-0.0
Rosenthal 22-69-0.0
Royal Bareuth 22-73-0.0
Royale 22-77-0.0
Royale Germania 22-81-0.0
Schmid 22-85-0.0

26 GREAT BRITAIN
Royal Doulton 26-69-0.0
Royal Worcester 26-78-0.0
Spode 26-86-0.0
Wedgwood 26-90-0.0

34 IRELAND
Belleek 34-8-0.0

38 ITALY
Anri 38-4-0.0
Kings 38-43-0.0
Studio Dante di Volteradici 38-72-0.0
Veneto Flair 38-84-0.0

42 JAPAN
Sango 42-72-0.0
Schmid 42-85-0.0

54 NORWAY
Porsgrund 54-61-0.0

72 SPAIN
Lladro 72-46-0.0
Santa Clara 72-72-0.0

76 SWEDEN
Orrefors 76-57-0.0
Rorstrand 76-69-0.0

84 UNITED STATES
Franklin Mint 84-23-0.0
Gorham 84-27-0.0
International 84-34-0.0
Lake Shore Prints 84-46-0.0
Lenox 84-50-0.0
Pickard 84-60-0.0
Reed & Barton 84-66-0.0
Rockwell Society 84-70-0.0
Royal Devon 84-74-0.0
Royal Worcester 84-78-0.0
Vernonware 84-84-0.0

APPENDICES
GLOSSARY OF COMMONLY
  USED TERMS A-1
INDEX OF PLATE MAKERS
  AND SPONSORS A-6
INDEX OF PLATE SERIES
  BY TYPE AND NAME A-7
INDEX OF PLATE TITLES A-9
INDEX OF ARTISTS A-15
ACKNOWLEDGEMENTS A-18

ARRANGEMENT OF THE LISTINGS

The Bradford Book of Collector's Plates is the official directory of all major issues regularly traded in the market. It is used to locate and identify all plates quickly and accurately. The plates are arranged by:

COUNTRY of origin in alphabetical order.
PLATE MAKER within each country, also in alphabetical order.
PLATE SERIES of each maker in chronological order beginning with the maker's first series.
INDIVIDUAL PLATES in each series, also in chronological order beginning with the first plate.

To speed identification, each plate is listed by its "Bradex" number. *THESE NUMBERS ARE IN SEQUENCE BUT NOT CONSECUTIVE.* The number on the upper outer corner of each page indicates the first plate listed on that page.

THE "BRADEX" NUMBER
of a plate is made up of four numbers.

(This number indicates the 1904 Bing & Grondahl Christmas plate)

14-8-1.10

COUNTRY
The first number indicates the country of origin. The number "**14**" is for Denmark. A list of countries with their "Bradex" numbers is in the Table of Contents on page **I-5**.

MAKER
The second number indicates the plate maker. The number "**8**" is for Bing & Grondahl. A list of makers with their "Bradex" numbers is in the Table of Contents on page **I-5**.

SERIES
The third number indicates the maker's series, listed in chronological order. The number "**1**" is for Bing & Grondahl's first series, the Christmas series. A list of series by type and name with their "Bradex" numbers is in the indexes on page **A-7**.

PLATE
The fourth number indicates the individual plate within each series, listed in chronological order. The number "**10**" is for the tenth plate in the Bing & Grondahl Christmas series, *View of Copenhagen from Fredericksberg Hill,* the 1904. A list of plate titles with their "Bradex" numbers is in the indexes on page **A-9**.

"Bradex" numbers are indexed by *Maker, Series Names and Types, Plate Titles* and *Artists* following the complete listing of plates.

LOCATION OF OTHER INFORMATION

Information on history, trademarks, artists, diameters, hanging provisions, edition limits, numbering, and issue price is included in each maker's listing. The listings are complete to 1976 issues, except where the maker did not supply photos before presstime. Typical edition limits given by makers in the listings may be defined as follows:

"Limited by edition size of 10,000" means only 10,000 plates were issued in the edition, and each plate was numbered.

"Limited by announced edition size of 10,000" means only 10,000 plates were issued in the edition, and plates were not numbered.

"Limited by announced period of issue" means the edition was limited to the number of plates produced during an announced time period.

"Limited by year of issue" means the edition was limited to the number of plates produced during the year of issue.

A Glossary of Commonly Used Terms is provided immediately following the listings.

THE WORLD'S MOST TRADED ART

by J. Roderick MacArthur
Director of the Board of Governors
of the Bradford Exchange

This year, as I went through my records for this Introduction to *The Bradford Book of Collector's Plates,* I was struck by one overriding fact:

Collector's plates — humble or glorious as you choose — have now become indisputedly *the most widely collected form of art in America.*

(And perhaps we can extend this to mean the world since more art probably is collected in America than anywhere else.)

Best estimates at the end of 1975 placed the number of plate collectors in the United States at 1,750,000 — and growing — without counting hundreds of thousands more who casually own collector's plates but do not yet think of themselves as "collectors". A study conducted by the Bradford Exchange late in 1974 projected 4,500,000 collectors by the end of 1978, and there has since been no reason to change that prediction (although some think it's too conservative).

The largest identifiable concentration of collectors — some 750,000 in the United States and 14 other countries — is served by the Bradford Exchange which is the largest single trading center for collector's plates in the world. At the end of 1975, transactions on the Exchange averaged 3,000 a day and continued to increase. No other form of art anywhere is traded in such volume.

So, if the official *Bradford Book of Collector's Plates* didn't exist, it would simply be necessary to invent it. To more and more serious collectors it is the single, indispensable, standard reference.

The *Book* is the only place where every plate in the mainstream of the market is classified with precision by maker, artist, edition limit, series and year. Such a continuing straightforward cataloging by "Bradex" number is a necessity for the quick, but thorough, identification of all 859 plates currently traded. (The Bradex number after each plate mentioned here tells you where it is in the *Book.*)

THE ROMANTIC MARKET

Some have said this makes the *Book* boring, with no "romance" about the plates listed. For this I take full blame but believe you will agree with my reasons.

One is simply that the market in these plates is so spectacularly "romantic" by itself that no further embellishment is needed. Over the past decade as the "hobby" has been expanding to every corner of the country, nothing has risen so dramatically as these market prices. Stories of huge profits have been commonplace. People who bought the Lalique Annual ("Bradex" number (**18-46-1.1**) in 1965, the Bing & Grondahl Mother's Day (**14-8-3.1**) in 1969, the Royal Doulton Mother's Day (**26-69-2.1**) in 1973, the Haviland Parlon Mother's Day (**18-32-3.1**) in 1975, have seen their plates multiply in price by 375% to 7000%! And literally scores of others have at least doubled in value.

In 1972 all of us at the Exchange noticed two things about the plate market: that despite the setbacks of that year it was fundamentally strong and growing stronger, and that nowhere was there an authoritative book that collectors could rely on for complete, factual information on the hundreds of plates that were already being traded.

I searched bookstores and found a few "guides" but discovered that none contained straightforward facts. They were filled with "lovely" and "priceless" plates, cluttered with "personal" favorites never really traded, and gave "current market prices" that were hopelessly out of date before they got off the press.

NO "LOVELY" PLATES

That was when we laid down some eventual "rules" for the *Bradford Book of Collector's Plates:*

There would be no "lovely" plates. The beauty of a plate's design would be left to the judgement of the collector.

There would be no "priceless" plates. If a plate is traded, it has a price.

There would be no "personal" favorites. If a plate is a favorite with collectors, that too will be reflected in the market trading, the only true reason for listing.

And there would be, above all, no misleading attempt to give "current market prices". For these, the market moves so quickly that you must consult a dealer or the Exchange quotations published six times a year.

So the *Bradford Book* contains only "issue" prices. You won't find a plate called "lovely" or "priceless" anywhere in its pages. You won't find someone's "favorite" plate that was once quickly promoted and just as quickly forgotten. You won't find a plate issued to commemorate the anniversary of your bank, your school, or even your state (and there have been many). You won't even find more than six of the scores of plates that have been issued for this year's Bicentennial; only these six are regularly traded in the market.

And you won't find listed any of the plates known as "supermarket plates" and "coterie plates". As the name implies, supermarket plates are sold in supermarkets, discount or chain stores. They are poorly made, have practically no artistic value, and are limited only by the manufacturer's idea of how many he can sell. They imitate collector's plates but are not at all the same thing.

Coterie plates, on the other hand, can be true collector's plates but made in such a small or obscure edition that in today's vastly expanded market they will remain unknown except to a small coterie of collectors.

A plate is listed on the Exchange, and in the *Book*, by the volume of continued trading — either past or expected — *not* by whether or not it will increase in market price. A new plate is listed before trading begins if it continues a series already traded. And a new series from a maker whose other series are widely traded may be listed if demand is expected to carry over to the new series.

The "Bradex" number by which each plate is listed here is how it is coded on the Exchange and immediately identifies it by country of origin, maker, series and plate number. (See page **I-6** for an explanation of these numbers.)

ONE SHAPE FOR ALL KINDS

In case you're new to the subject, collector's plates bear pictures or sculpture and are made in various sizes but mainly in only one shape: round. A few plates have been introduced in squarish shapes, but so far only two, the Royal Doulton ("Bradex" number **(26-69-1.0)** and Rorstrand **(76-69-1.0)** Christmas series, have "made the Bradex", that is, have been listed on the Exchange.

Nearly all listed plates can be considered handmade (although some are more so than others), and many are completely handpainted.

They can be made in wafer-thin china like the Belleek of Ireland **(34-8-0.0)** or in massive sculptured stone like the Di Volteradici of Italy **(38-72-0.0)**. They can be metal (mainly silver, silverplate, and pewter), crystal, even wood like the Anri **(38-4-0.0)**. But most are made in ceramics, from simple terra cotta to true hard-fire porcelain.

Most can be used as dinner plates but rarely ever are. Instead you'll find them hanging on the walls of museums and placed with great pride in little stands on grandmothers' side tables. They are sold in department stores, gift shops, specialty shops and antique stores. Some few like the D'Arceau-Limoges "Women of the Century" **(18-15-3.0)** can only be imported one by one from abroad by private invitation.

And always you find them moving with their changing prices on and off the floor of the Exchange. Here, however, they are merely represented by thousands of pieces of paper, called "buy-orders" and "sell-orders", changing hands without an actual plate in sight. The action is fast, and the rewards can be great if you win. (But don't be too tempted to speculate. Wait 'till I tell you what happened to some pretty smart speculators in 1972.)

EDITION LIMITS AND MARKET VALUE

One thing all collector's plates have in common, of course, is that they are "limited editions".

There has been much debate as to what this means since some manufacturers give the precise number in their editions while others, particularly those with the widest following, insist that it be kept a deep, dark secret forever.

But there is one thing you can be sure of: With only one exception*, *no plate in the* Bradford Book *(or traded on the Exchange) has ever been reissued once the edition is closed.*

The range between edition sizes is vast. the smallest *announced* edition limit listed in the *Bradford Book* is 250 for the 1971 Royal Germania Mother's Day **(28-91-2.0)**; the largest is 30,000 for the Haviland Christmas **(18-30-1.0)**. But the *undisclosed* editions are far the largest, ranging from less than 1,000 for the earliest editions into the hundreds of thousands for the later ones.

Time was, when the market was small, a new plate series in an edition of 2,000 or less could become established and sometimes trade up in price to dizzying heights. Today, with the market so vastly expanded, it is unlikely this can ever happen again. A brand new series launched with an edition of less than 10,000 would probably remain unknown except as a coterie plate.

So don't let me discourage you from adding an obscure plate you really like to your collection, but *don't expect it to go up in market value* just because the edition is small. The market value of a plate is *never* determined by the size of the edition alone; it is by the *ratio* of supply to demand, and a very small an edition can't create much demand.

OPEN-ENDED; CLOSE-ENDED

Most plates are produced in *series* — either "close-ended" in a pre-determined number of editions, such as the D'Arceau-Limoges "Noel Vitrail" Christmas series **(18-15-2.0)**, scheduled for eight editions, or "open-ended" to continue indefinitely, such as the Bing and Grondahl Christmas series **(14-8-1.0)**. Most collectors specialize in one or more of these series. (In fact, they probably *must* specialize in something; there are 859 listed plates in this book, and I have yet to hear of a collector who has them all.)

The first plate in a series is often — but not always — the most wanted. Some collectors refer to these plates as "first editions", but this is a misnomer. Practically all plates listed are first editions since an edition

---

*The one exception is the Rosenthal Traditional Christmas series **(22-69-1.0)**. Editions from 1910 to 1971 in this series were reopened briefly between 1969 and 1971. But these plates are now "Bradex listed" on the firm assurance by the maker that the practice ceased forever in 1971, thus making them "limited editions" at last, and on a determination by the Board of the Exchange that current prices now reflect all plates in the editions regardless of when they were made.

One other well known plate was "delisted" in 1974 when a second, "European" edition appeared with no indication that it was not the original edition released in the United States. "Over-the-counter" trading fell off, and this delisting may become permanent.

WORLD'S MOST TRADED ART

I-9

is never repeated; the first in a series is called a *first issue*.

THE UNEXPLAINED PHENOMENON

I suppose it was inevitable — as these plates have gradually become the most widely collected form of art and prices for the prized editions outstripped the most glamorous stocks and bonds — for a host of amateur sociologists to arise among collectors and dealers to try to explain this fabulous phenomenon in our society. At any rate, we have not lacked for "explanations", all comparing collector's plates to other fields and I believe, all failing to explain them very well.

Bing & Grondahl, the very oldest manufacturer — who should be the best authority — says that they are "closely connected with the traditions of interior decorating." While plates can certainly decorate an interior, to suggest this as their primary function is to lose any hint of the joyful acquisition, the searching, bidding and trading that collectors delight in — to lose the whole idea of collecting at all.

Others who suggest that collector's plates are "giftware" bring us no closer to an answer. Of course, collector's plates make fine gifts — that's what they were *before* they were collector's plates — but again, we are not *collecting* merely by giving or receiving a gift.

But what is most confusing — and most widespread — is the comparison with antiques.

A surprising number of dealers, manufacturers and collectors — all of whom should know better — persist in suggesting that plates can somehow become "instant" antiques. It is easy to see how some people might perfer plates to antiques because the former are so easily identified, usually right on the plate itself. Even the danger of copies and counterfeits is close to non-existent. (I know of only one counterfeit, that of the famous 1962 Royal Copenhagen "Little Mermaid" **(14-69-1.55)** made in Portugal, and fortunately the counterfeit is so crude it is easy to distinguish from the real thing.) But not even the oldest collector's plates are yet old enough to be considered antiques by the generally accepted definition, and the fast-moving market in plates can hardly compare with the slow, involved trading in antiques.

Still others compare plate collecting with stamp collecting and coin collecting — and there are comfortable similarities: a defined national market with fast-changing prices and occasional wild speculation. But there, I think, the similarities end. No plate collector would compare the art of his plate with the art that appears on a stamp or coin. And, in fact, art has virtually no bearing on the value of a stamp or coin. Both are normally hidden away in albums while collector's plates are intended for display.

And there is a most vital difference: no stamp or coin is normally issued as a limited edition; it becomes so only after it is discontinued.

The comparisons with other forms of art are little better. There is not the same uniform, codified market in other art and no continuous trading between the occasional, spectacular auctions.

So the closest comparison to the continuous trading in plates is that of stocks and bonds. Of course, many plates are collected as an investment, but, unlike stocks and bonds, they are not collected *only* as an investment; this would ignore art entirely.

In most respects, plates cannot be compared with stocks and bonds. Stocks are rarely reflected in the plate market; when stocks fall, plates go up. In early 1973, the Bradford Exchange was declared to be dealing in unregistered securities by the U.S. Securities and Exchange Commission when it guaranteed that one plate series would double in value (which it did). Since then, the official view of the Exchange is that if collector's plates are to be considered investments, they should be considered commodities, not securities, preferably art commodities, and modern art at that.

THE STANDARD YARDSTICK

And there is no denying that many plate editions have, in fact, been spectacular investments. But what's the secret? How do you know which plates will succeed and which will fall by the wayside?

To my knowledge, no one knows. However, in 1972, the Bradford Exchange did compile an eight-point checklist for evaluation of any plate. Since then it has become something of a standard yardstick:

1. **ARTISTRY:** Is it original art created especially for this plate by a living artist of note? Is the subject one of broad appeal but not trite?
2. **MAKER:** Is the maker known for fine workmanship and continuity?
3. **RARITY:** Is it a first edition? Is it tightly limited yet not too limited to create a market? If the edition is closed, are dealers bidding in the secondary market?
4. **COLLECTIBILITY:** Is it one, preferably the first, of a collectible periodic series or merely a single issue?
5. **TIME OF ACQUISITION:** Can you acquire it at the right time — at issue, or while the price is still rising?
6. **MATERIAL:** If made of metal, is it solid gold or silver? If made of glass, is it genuine 24% lead crystal? If made of ceramic, is it true hard-paste (or "hard-fire") porcelain, bone china or fine china?
7. **SPONSORSHIP:** Is it issued by a government or an official non-profit institution?
8. **COMMEMORATIVE IMPORTANCE:** Does it commemorate a seasonal event or an historic event? If so, does it bring new insight to the event? Or is it an event in the history of the artist, or of the maker?

These points were originally intended to be in order of importance. Personally, however, I would reverse the first two: the record of the MAKER (2) seems to be even more important in the market than the point of ARTISTRY (1). RARITY (3) and COLLECTIBILITY (4) are, of course, important, but I would put SPONSORSHIP (7), which is quite rare, well ahead of MATERIAL (6) which was more important in the days when silver plates were riding high. Perhaps material should now even come after COMMEMORATIVE IMPORTANCE (8). TIME OF ACQUISITION (5) has to do with the price itself and its importance is obvious: if you pay too much for a plate, you may take years to break even. Yet even at a high aftermarket price, a plate can be a bargain if it's still going up.

OBSCURE CHRISTMAS CUSTOM

And to think that all of this excitement involving millions of people can be traced to a small blue and white plate issued in Denmark 81 years ago.

Every history ever written about collector's plates agrees that this first plate was made by Bing & Grondahl. Two semi-official histories say it was inspired by an old Danish custom of giving decorated wooden plates to the common folk at Christmas time. This is a nice idea, but to the best of my knowledge, no one has ever seen one of these wooden plates that supposedly represented such a widespread custom.

Bing & Grondahl says instead that the custom had its beginning in the Renaissance when an honored guest was given the plates from which he had eaten his meal. This suggests the rather unlikely scene of a nobleman coming home from dinner with a large, clanking "doggie bag" full of tableware.

Whatever the truth of the custom (and I must admit I, too, can't clarify it any further), Mr. Harald Bing, the younger of the Bing Brothers, did, in fact, issue the first collector's plate in 1895 **(14-8-1.1)**. He was the first to identify the plate as a Christmas plate with the year of manufacture on the front. But it is doubtful that Mr. Bing thought of the now-famous "Frozen Window" plate as a limited edition. More probably he merely thought he could not sell an 1895 plate in 1896.

Bing & Grondahl claims to have kept secret the number of plates produced each year, but knowledgeable estimates are that about 400 of the historic 1895 plates were made. I believe the majority of these still exist, most as part of complete collections of the Bing & Grondahl Christmas series, and most now in the United States. The plates, which originally sold for about 50¢, now trade at around $3,000 on the exchange.

In her book, *Modern Porcelain* (Harper & Rowe, 1962), Alberta Tremble tells us the plate was issued to commemorate the reorganization of the Bing & Grondahl Company and the opening of its new, greatly enlarged plant. I must correct, however, Ms. Tremble's claim that "the plates caught on like wild fire. Potters everywhere copied the idea." In fact, Royal Copenhagen did not copy the idea until 1908

Harald Bing

(14-69-1.1), 13 years later. Porsgrund in Norway tried it in 1909 but abandoned it for lack of success. Rorstrand in Sweden began in 1904 and hung on until 1926 when they, too, gave up. (Both Porsgrund **(54-61-1.0)** and Rorstrand **(76-69-1.0)** were to begin production again in 1968, but only after the American market had developed.)

However, like the Bing & Grondahl, the original Royal Copenhagen series did survive, and the two Danish rivals still command the largest total share of the market.

Although these early Christmas plates are now true collector's plates as we understand them, they were not at the time. Danish families did collect them, of course, but only a single year at a time, and occasionally a year or two was skipped. They had no thought that one edition might be more valuable than another, and the idea of a complete collection was yet to come.

As Danes emigrated to the United States they brought collector's plates with them. But until the late 1940s the plates were little known in America except in a few antique shops, most of them in Scandinavian neighborhoods. Only two importers, Georg Jensen (who later became a plate maker) and Stanley Cocoran, were importing plates for transplanted Danes.

It seems difficult to imagine today that the earliest American dealers entered into the collector's plate market with no idea at all what they were starting.

"If you had told me in 1947 that someday there would be millions of plate collectors, I just wouldn't have believed you," says Chicago antique dealer William Freudenberg, Jr., today. Yet in 1947, he became the very first to recognize the possibilities in the Danish plates when he began reselling them to other

William Freudenberg, Jr.

Patricia Owen

WORLD'S MOST TRADED ART

antique dealers. "I simply found them at an auction house," he says, "and took a few to see what I could do." His price for the oldest Bing & Grondahls at that time was only $4.50 (the same plates that bring up to $3,000 in the market at this writing).

In 1949, Patricia Owen in Fort Lauderdale, Florida, became a dealer through a fluke. An American company wanted to sell cash registers in Denmark, but exporting Danish currency was prohibited. To get around this the company used the Danish kroners to buy collector's plates from young Danes, who had lost all interest in their family's collections, and resold them for American dollars to Ms. Owens. She became the first dealer to sell plates to gift shops and department stores.

That same year, the Rev. Elias Rasmussen, a Norwegian-born pastor from Minneapolis, was traveling in Denmark when he met an elderly lady who was trying to sell her plates. No one in Denmark wanted them at any price; so the Rev. Mr. Rasmussen brought them back to America to see if he could sell them for her here. Within a few years he was selling plates by the thousands, and his son, Roland, continued the business after his death.

In 1950 Jon Nielsen settled in Dearborn, Michigan and began importing the Danish plates along with antiques from the old country. He sold them all for about $3.50 apiece regardless of the year of issue.

"Not until 1953 did dealers want any current plates," he says. "The next year I raised my prices to $3.75, and you should have heard them complain that I was charging too much."

But the thing that really moved collector's plates out of the realm of antiques and giftware took place in 1951. Svend Jensen in Rye, New York, began importing Danish plates in 1950 and was the first to decide to charge different prices for different back issues. In 1951 he printed the first back-issue price list based on his estimate of the scarcity of each edition — and the modern market in collector's plates was born.

Antique dealers and gift shops around the country began quoting Svend Jensen's prices, and other price lists began to appear. Collectors with recent issues tried to complete their collections with earlier plates. Prices were bid up well beyond Svend Jensen's early lists; yet as late as 1955 the most prized Bing & Grondahl plate from 1895 could still be bought for only $75.

By 1960 with the supply of antiques dwindling and more and more plate collectors asking for current editions of the Danish Christmas plates, antique dealers began to sell the new editions even though they could not be considered antiques. New editions also began to appear in more and more specialty gift shops. Customers buying for the first time began looking for earlier issues, and a circular demand began from one kind of dealer to another.

In 1962 demand from Americans who had visited Copenhagen, transplanted Danes, the growing army of plate collectors and many people who had simply fallen in love with the Hans Christian Andersen story centered on the Royal Copenhagen Christmas plate, "The Little Mermaid" **(14-69-1.55)**. Issued at about $11, it immediately began to rise in market price, which tended to increase prices for all earlier editions. Although many thousands were made, it traded at around $200 early this year.

CRYSTAL SHATTERS MARKET

In 1965 Lalique of France, whose crystalware was selling in shops where Danish plates were unheard of, brought out the first of its annual crystal plates "Deux Oiseaux" **(18-46-1.1)**. This shattered the boundaries of plate collecting as then known because it was not porcelain, it was not Danish, and it was not even a Christmas plate. It was simply called an "annual" and finally set the stage for limited-edition plates as true "collector's items".

When Bing & Grondahl issued the first Mother's Day plate, "Dog and Puppies", in 1969 **(14-8-3.1)**, collectors scrambled to buy it at the issue price of $9.75. They knew that earlier Bing & Grondahl Christmas plates were selling at many times issue prices and bought the new plate as an outright investment. The issue sold out quickly and went up in price, again pushing other back-issue prices even higher. Later that year, Wedgwood of England issued its first Christmas plate, "Windsor Castle" **(26-90-1.1)**; it, too, sold out quickly and began to climb in value. Suddenly it seemed as though everyone was joining the stampede.

To meet the newly discovered demand, plate makers entered the field from far and near. Svend Jensen decided to make his own plates; so did Haviland, Belleek, Spode, Kaiser, Berlin, Lenox, Santa Clara, Pickard, Reed

Elias Rasmussen

Jon Nielsen

& Barton and Orrefors, among others; all were successful and still survive. Franklin Mint made history by issuing the first silver collector's plate, Norman Rockwell's "Bringing Home the Tree" **(84-23-1.1)**, and it too was a runaway success. Prices of editions increased as soon as they closed, with demand coming from more and more avid collectors.

In 1971 still more new makers like Furstenberg, Gorham and Lladro entered the market. Haviland Parlon **(18-32-1.0)** began a series patterned after medieval tapestries, Goebel **(22-27-1.0)** introduced plates based on their famous Hummel figurines, and Veneto Flair **(38-84-0.0)** began a series of handmade plates from Italy. Older makes like Royal Copenhagen and Wedgwood introduced new Mothers Day series.

Svend Jensen

Even this new surge in supply did not keep up with demand. As the number of collectors and dealers increased, prices continued to rise. News of the boom began to appear in the press. In December 1971, an article appeared in the *Wall Street Journal* under the headline "While You Were Going Under, Granny Got In at $100, Got Out at $450". This was based on the spectacular price rise of the first Franklin Mint Christmas plate, and among other plates, reporter Scott R. Schmedel singled out the 1969 Wedgwood Christmas plate which had been issued at $25 and was then selling for about $200. To show this could be momentary inflation, he quoted a serious Wedgwood collector as predicting its value would fall back and stabilize around $80. Instead, it has held its price ever since and even traded as high as $300. This article and others like it were widely reprinted and set the stage for 1972 as the year of the speculator.

That year more and more makers entered the market: plates of poor design and quality were rushed into production. Thousands of new dealers and collectors began speculating with little or no study of plates or of the market. New "mints" sprang up to grind out silver plates on the heels of Franklin Mint's success.

Finally one mint advertised its silver "collie" with pictures of an acid-etched plate and sold thousands before it was produced. Prices rose dramatically, but the actual plate was stamped, not etched, and collectors began turning away. Another new mint introduced six new silver plates at once.

Suddenly dealers all over the country were overstocked and prices for silver plates fell below issue. All other plates began to fall on the heels of the silver crash: dealers panicked, and the speculator-collectors, many of whom had tried to become "bedroom dealers", saw their visions of quick riches vanish.

After the "crash of 1972 as the year of the speculator, 1973 became the year of the "shake-out". Several "mints" closed their doors, thousands of plates were melted back into silver, established makers cut back production dramatically, and the bedroom dealers faded from the scene.

But the number of collectors continued to grow. Thousands entered the market to buy two spectacular series begun that year: The Lafayette Legacy Collection from D'Arceau-Limoges **(18-15-1.0)** was unavailable to dealers but imported by individual collectors directly from France and widely traded on the secondary market, and "Collette and Child" **(26-69-2.1)** from Royal Doulton was the first plate by celebrated artist Edna Hibel. While marginal plates disappeared from trading, established plates remained steady and slowly regained their market strength.

Then, in 1974, a new phenomenon began: as news of the American plate collecting boom spread slowly abroad, plates that originated in Europe but had never found a market there — such as the Rosenthal Wiinblad **(26-69-2.0)** and the Rorstrand Christmas **(76-69-1.0)** series — began being bid up in the American Market by foreign dealers to sell back in Europe. This was the first reversal of the previous trend, and it has continued.

MARKET MATURES

Since 1974, the overall "Market Bradex", the sort of Dow Jones index of collector's plate prices, has shown a steady increase that bodes well for the future. Hundreds of thousands of new collectors have come into the market each year while the older collectors have become more selective. Quality of material and workmanship, as well as artistry, has improved. Although average gains have been perhaps less breathtaking than during the boom of 1971, they have long since wiped out the losses of 1972 and are spread over more than half again as many plates listed since then. And a few new editions like the first Rockwell Society Christmas plate **(84-70-1.0)** or the 1975 Haviland Parlon Mother's Day **(18-32-2.4)** can still double within a year of issue.

So the heady prospect of spectacular profits is still with us in 1976, and steady growth looks rather sure for the years to come.

DIRECTORY OF PLATES

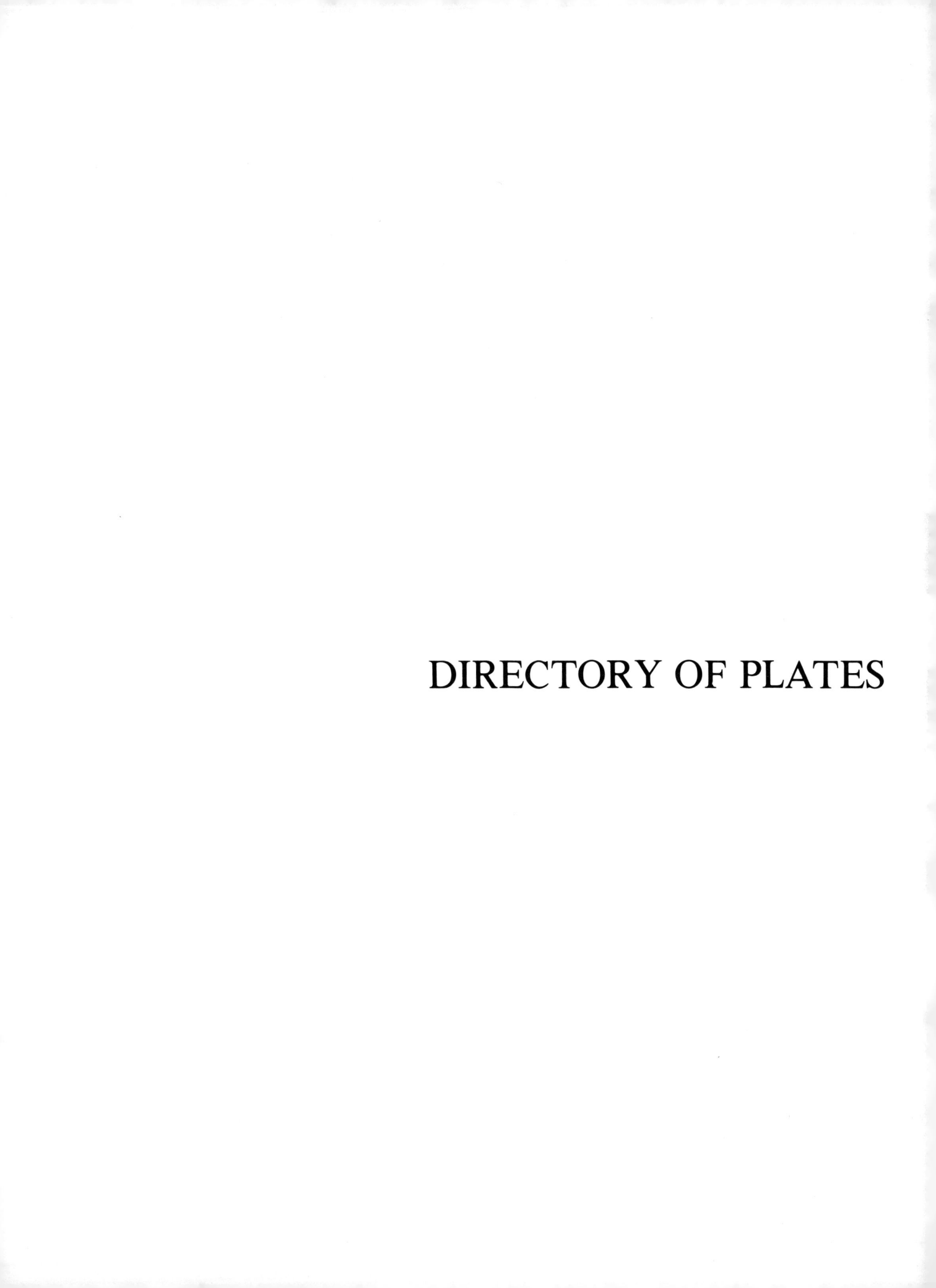

4-61-1.1
PORCELANA GRANADA (Rosario)

ARGENTINA

Since 1972, the Porcelana Granada series of Christmas plates has been made by one of Argentina's largest porcelain factories, Porcelana Verbano. (The 1971 plate was produced in Cali, Colombia.) Porcelana Verbano is a recognized producer of dinnerware and hand-painted pieces. The Christmas series, *Pax in Terra,* based on the life of Christ, was begun in 1971 and is to run 15 years.

All plates listed are made in porcelain and decorated in cobalt blue. Diameter: 7 inches. Foot rims pierced for hanging. Numbered since 1972 without certificate.

Christmas Series

4-61-1.1
1971 *The Annunciation.*
Artist: Tom Fennell, Jr. Limited by announced edition size of 9,300.
Issue price: $12.00

4-61-1.2
1972 *Mary and Elizabeth.*
Artist: Gerry Sparks. Limited by edition size of 6,000. Issue price: $13.00

4-61-1.3
1973 *Road to Bethlehem.*
Artist: Gerry Sparks. Limited by edition size of 5,000. Issue price: $14.00

4-61-1.4
1974 *No Room at the Inn.*
Artist: Gerry Sparks. Limited by edition size of 5,000. Issue price: $15.00

4-61-1.5
1975 *Shepherds in the Field.*
Artist: Gerry Sparks. Limited by edition size of 5,000. Issue price: $16.50

4-61-1.6
1976 *The Nativity.*
Artist: Gerry Sparks. Limited by edition size of 5,000. Issue price: $17.50

DENMARK
BING & GRONDAHL (Copenhagen)

14-8-1.1

Established in 1853, Bing & Grondahl is Denmark's second oldest existing porcelain maker (after Royal Copenhagen). Frederik Vilhelm Grondahl, who supplied the artistic ideas, was a young sculptor previously employed by The Royal Copenhagen Porcelain Manufactory. M. H. and J. H. Bing, prosperous businessmen, provided financial backing. In 1895, Bing & Grondahl issued the world's first recognized collector's plate. This began its Christmas series which has been produced each year without interruption despite wars and economic crises. Plates in this series are the most widely collected and most frequently traded of all plates in the market. A second series, the *Jubilee* plates, was begun in 1915, and repeats past Christmas editions in larger size every five years. A Mother's Day series was introduced in 1969. The artist is Henry Thelander. Bing & Grondahl makes many other porcelain articles (including other limited-edition plates that have not become listed collector's plates) in various styles.

All plates listed are made in porcelain in bas-relief and are hand-painted in "Copenhagen blue" using the true underglaze technique. Each plate is initialed on the back by its painter. Foot rims pierced for hanging. Limited by year of issue. Edition size undisclosed. Not numbered.

Christmas Series
Diameter: 7 inches.

14-8-1.1
1895 *Behind the Frozen Window.*
Artist: F. A. Hallin. Issue price: $.50

14-8-1.2
1896 *New Moon over Snow-covered Trees.*
Artist: F. A. Hallin. Issue price: $.50

14-8-1.3
1897 *Christmas Meal of the Sparrows.*
Artist: F. A. Hallin. Issue price: $.75

14-8-1.4
1898 *Christmas Roses and Christmas Star.*
Artist: Fanny Garde. Issue price: $.75

14-8-1.5
1899 *The Crows Enjoying Christmas.*
Artist: Dahl Jensen. Issue Price: $.75

14-8-1.6
1900 *Church Bells Chiming in Christmas.*
Artist: Dahl Jensen. Issue price: $.75

14-8-1.7
1901 *The Three Wise Men from the East.*
Artist: S. Sabra. Issue price: $1.00

14-8-1.8
1902 *Interior of a Gothic Church.*
Artist: Dahl Jensen. Issue price: $1.00

14-8-1.9

DENMARK
BING & GRONDAHL

14-8-1.9
1903 *Happy Expectation of Children.*
Artist: Margrethe Hyldahl. Issue price: $1.00

14-8-1.10
1904 *View of Copenhagen from Frederiksberg Hill.*
Artist: Cathinka Olsen. Issue price: $1.00

14-8-1.11
1905 *Anxiety of the Coming Christmas Night.*
Artist: Dahl Jensen. Issue price: $1.00

14-8-1.12
1906 *Sleighing to Church on Christmas Eve.*
Artist: Dahl Jensen. Issue price: $1.00

14-8-1.13
1907 *The Little Match Girl.*
Artist: E. Plockross. Issue price: $1.00

14-8-1.14
1908 *St. Petri Church of Copenhagen.*
Artist: Povl Jorgensen. Issue price: $1.00

14-8-1.15
1909 *Happiness over the Yule Tree.*
Artist: Aarestrup. Issue price: $1.50

14-8-1.16
1910 *The Old Organist.*
Artist: C. Ersgaard. Issue price: $1.50

14-8-1.17
1911 *First It Was Sung by Angels to Shepherds in the Fields.*
Artist: H. Moltke. Issue price: $1.50

14-8-1.18
1912 *Going to Church on Christmas Eve.*
Artist: Einar Hansen. Issue price: $1.50

14-8-1.19
1913 *Bringing Home the Yule Tree.*
Artist: Th. Larsen. Issue price: $1.50

14-8-1.20
1914 *Royal Castle of Amalienborg, Copenhagen.*
Artist: Th. Larsen. Issue price: $1.50

DENMARK
BING & GRONDAHL

14-8-1.21

14-8-1.21
1915 *Chained Dog Getting Double Meal on Christmas Eve.*
Artist: Dahl Jensen. Issue price: $1.50

14-8-1.22
1916 *Christmas Prayer of the Sparrows.*
Artist: J. Bloch Jorgensen. Issue price: $1.50

14-8-1.23
1917 *Arrival of the Christmas Boat.*
Artist: Achton Friis. Issue price: $1.50

14-8-1.24
1918 *Fishing Boat Returning Home for Christmas.*
Artist: Achton Friis. Issue price: $1.50

14-8-1.25
1919 *Outside the Lighted Window.*
Artist: Achton Friis. Issue price: $2.00

14-8-1.26
1920 *Hare in the Snow.*
Artist: Achton Friis. Issue price: $2.00

14-8-1.27
1921 *Pigeons in the Castle Court.*
Artist: Achton Friis. Issue price: $2.00

14-8-1.28
1922 *Star of Bethlehem.*
Artist: Achton Friis. Issue price: $2.00

14-8-1.29
1923 *Royal Hunting Castle, the Ermitage.*
Artist: Achton Friis. Issue price: $2.00

14-8-1.30
1924 *Lighthouse in Danish Waters.*
Artist: Achton Friis. Issue price: $2.50

14-8-1.31
1925 *The Child's Christmas.*
Artist: Achton Friis. Issue price: $2.50

14-8-1.32
1926 *Churchgoers on Christmas Day.*
Artist: Achton Friis. Issue price: $2.50

14-8-1.33

DENMARK
BING & GRONDAHL

14-8-1.33
1927 *Skating Couple.*
Artist: Achton Friis. Issue price: $2.50

14-8-1.34
1928 *Eskimos Looking at Village Church in Greenland.*
Artist: Achton Friis. Issue price: $2.50

14-8-1.35
1929 *Fox Outside Farm on Christmas Eve.*
Artist: Achton Friis. Issue price: $2.50

14-8-1.36
1930 *Yule Tree in Town Hall Square of Copenhagen.*
Artist: H. Flugenring. Issue price: $2.50

14-8-1.37
1931 *Arrival of the Christmas Train.*
Artist: Achton Friis. Issue price: $2.50

14-8-1.38
1932 *Lifeboat at Work.*
Artist: H. Flugenring. Issue price: $2.50

14-8-1.39
1933 *The Korsor-Nyborg Ferry.*
Artist: H. Flugenring. Issue price: $3.00

14-8-1.40
1934 *Church Bell in Tower.*
Artist: Immanuel Tjerne. Issue price: $3.00

14-8-1.41
1935 *Lillebelt Bridge Connecting Funen with Jutland.*
Artist: Ove Larsen. Issue price: $3.00

14-8-1.42
1936 *Royal Guard Outside Amalienborg Castle in Copenhagen.*
Artist: Ove Larsen. Issue price: $3.00

14-8-1.43
1937 *Arrival of Christmas Guests.*
Artist: Ove Larsen. Issue price: $3.00

14-8-1.44
1938 *Lighting the Candles.*
Artist: Immanuel Tjerne. Issue price: $3.00

DENMARK
BING & GRONDAHL

14-8-1.45

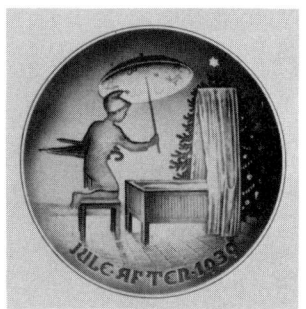

14-8-1.45
1939 *Ole Lock-Eye, the Sandman.*
Artist: Immanuel Tjerne. Issue price: $3.00

14-8-1.46
1940 *Delivering Christmas Letters.*
Artist: Ove Larsen. Issue price: $4.00

14-8-1.47
1941 *Horses Enjoying Christmas Meal in Stable.*
Artist: Ove Larsen. Issue price: $4.00

14-8-1.48
1942 *Danish Farm on Christmas Night.*
Artist: Ove Larsen. Issue price: $4.00

14-8-1.49
1943 *The Ribe Cathedral.*
Artist: Ove Larsen. Issue price: $5.00

14-8-1.50
1944 *Sorgenfri Castle.*
Artist: Ove Larsen. Issue price: $5.00

14-8-1.51
1945 *The Old Water Mill.*
Artist: Ove Larsen. Issue price: $5.00

14-8-1.52
1946 *Commemoration Cross in Honor of Danish Sailors Who Lost Their Lives in World War II.*
Artist: Margrethe Hyldahl. Issue price: $5.00

14-8-1.53
1947 *Dybbol Mill.*
Artist: Margrethe Hyldahl. Issue price: $5.00

14-8-1.54
1948 *Watchman, Sculpture of Town Hall, Copenhagen.*
Artist: Margrethe Hyldahl. Issue price: $5.50

14-8-1.55
1949 *Landsoldaten, 19th Century Danish Soldier.*
Artist: Margrethe Hyldahl. Issue price: $5.50

14-8-1.56
1950 *Kronborg Castle at Elsinore.*
Artist: Margrethe Hyldahl. Issue price: $5.50

14-8-1.57

DENMARK
BING & GRONDAHL

14-8-1.57
1951 *Jens Bang, New Passenger Boat Running Between Copenhagen and Aalborg.*
Artist: Margrethe Hyldahl. Issue price: $6.00

14-8-1.58
1952 *Old Copenhagen Canals at Wintertime, with Thorvaldsen Museum in Background.*
Artist: Borge Pramvig. Issue price: $6.00

14-8-1.59
1953 *Royal Boat in Greenland Waters.*
Artist: Kjeld Bonfils. Issue price: $7.00

14-8-1.60
1954 *Birthplace of Hans Christian Andersen, with Snowman.*
Artist: Borge Pramvig. Issue price: $7.50

14-8-1.61
1955 *Kalundborg Church.*
Artist: Kjeld Bonfils. Issue price: $8.00

14-8-1.62
1956 *Christmas in Copenhagen.*
Artist: Kjeld Bonfils. Issue price: $8.50

14-8-1.63
1957 *Christmas Candles.*
Artist: Kjeld Bonfils. Issue price: $9.00

14-8-1.64
1958 *Santa Claus.*
Artist: Kjeld Bonfils. Issue price: $9.50

14-8-1.65
1959 *Christmas Eve.*
Artist: Kjeld Bonfils. Issue price: $10.00

14-8-1.66
1960 *Danish Village Church.*
Artist: Kjeld Bonfils. Issue price: $10.00

14-8-1.67
1961 *Winter Harmony.*
Artist: Kjeld Bonfils. Issue price: $10.50

14-8-1.68
1962 *Winter Night.*
Artist: Kjeld Bonfils. Issue price: $11.00

DENMARK
BING & GRONDAHL

14-8-1.69

14-8-1.69
1963 *The Christma Elf.*
Artist: Henry Thelander. Issue price: $11.00

14-8-1.70
1964 *The Fir Tree and Hare.*
Artist: Henry Thelander. Issue price: $11.50

14-8-1.71
1965 *Bringing Home the Christmas Tree.*
Artist: Henry Thelander. Issue price: $12.00

14-8-1.72
1966 *Home for Christmas.*
Artist: Henry Thelander. Issue price: $12.00

14-8-1.73
1967 *Sharing the Joy of Christmas.*
Artist: Henry Thelander. Issue price: $13.00

14-8-1.74
1968 *Christmas in Church.*
Artist: Henry Thelander. Issue price: $14.00

14-8-1.75
1969 *Arrival of Christmas Guests.*
Artist: Henry Thelander. Issue price: $14.00

14-8-1.76
1970 *Pheasants in the Snow at Christmas.*
Artist: Henry Thelander. Issue price: $14.50

14-8-1.77
1971 *Christmas at Home.*
Artist: Henry Thelander. Issue price: $15.00

14-8-1.78
1972 *Christmas in Greenland.*
Artist: Henry Thelander. Issue price: $16.50

14-8-1.79
1973 *Family Reunion.*
Artist: Henry Thelander. Issue price: $19.50

14-8-1.80
1974 *Christmas in the Village.*
Artist: Henry Thelander. Issue price: $22.00

14-8-1.81

DENMARK
BING & GRONDAHL

14-8-1.81
1975 *The Old Water Mill.*
Artist: Henry Thelander. Issue price: $27.50

14-8-1.82
1976 *Christmas Welcome.*
Artist: Henry Thelander. Issue price: $27.50

Jubilee Series

Diameter: 9 inches

14-8-2.1
1915: From 1895 Christmas plate.
Issue price: $3.00

14-8-2.2
1920: From 1900 Christmas plate.
Issue price: $4.00

14-8-2.3
1925: From 1915 Christmas plate.
Issue price: $5.00

14-8-2.4
1930: From 1910 Christmas plate.
Issue price: $5.00

14-8-2.5
1935: From 1907 Christmas plate.
Issue price: $6.00

14-8-2.6
1940: From 1901 Christmas plate.
Issue price: $10.00

14-8-2.7
1945: From 1936 Christmas plate.
Issue price: $10.00

14-8-2.8
1950: From 1928 Christmas plate.
Issue price: $15.00

14-8-2.9
1955: From 1947 Christmas plate.
Issue price: $20.00

14-8-2.10
1960: From 1950 Christmas plate.
Issue price: $25.00

14-8-2.11
1965: From 1926 Christmas plate.
Issue price: $25.00

14-8-2.12
1970: From 1914 Christmas plate.
Issue price: $30.00

14-8-2.13
1975: From 1941 Christmas plate.
Issue price: $40.00

Mother's Day Series

Diameter: 6 inches

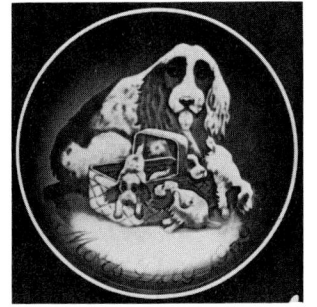

14-8-3.1
1969 *Dog and Puppies.*
Issue price: $9.75

14-8-3.2
1970 *Bird and Chicks.*
Issue price: $10.00

DENMARK
BING & GRONDAHL

14-8-3.3

14-8-3.3
1971 *Cat and Kittens.*
Issue price: $11.00

14-8-3.4
1972 *Mare and Foal.*
Issue price: $12.00

14-8-3.5
1973 *Duck and Ducklings.*
Issue price: $13.00

14-8-3.6
1974 *Bear and Cubs.*
Issue price: $16.50

14-8-3.7
1975 *Doe and Fawn.*
Issue price: $19.50

14-8-3.8
1976 *Swan Family.*
Issue price: $22.50

14-38-1.1
GEORG JENSEN (Copenhagen)

DENMARK

Georg Jensen, known primarily for Danish silver, issued its first annual porcelain Christmas plate in 1972, and in 1973 its first Mother's Day plate. Names of artists undisclosed.

All plates listed are made in porcelain in bas-relief and are hand-painted in "Copenhagen blue" using the true underglaze technique. Each plate is initialed on the back by its painter. Foot rims pierced for hanging. Limited by year of issue. Edition size undisclosed. Not numbered.

Christmas Series

Diameter: 7¼ inches

14-38-1.1
1972 *Doves.*
Issue price: $15.00

14-38-1.2
1973 *Boy and Dog on Christmas Eve.*
Issue price: $15.00

14-38-1.3
1974 *Christmas Story.*
Issue price: $17.50

14-38-1.4
1975 *Winter Scene.*
Issue price: $22.50

14-38-1.5
1976 *Christmas in the Country.*
Issue price: $22.50

DENMARK
GEORG JENSEN

14-38-2.1

Mother's Day Series
Diameter: 6¾ inches

14-38-2.1
1973 *Mother and Child.*
Issue price: $15.00

14-38-2.2
1974 *Sweet Dreams.*
Issue price: $17.50

14-38-2.3
1975 *A Mother's World.*
Issue price: $22.50

14-40-1.1
SVEND JENSEN (Ringsted)

DENMARK

Svend Jensen plates are made by the Desiree porcelain factory in Ringsted on the outskirts of Copenhagen. Both the Christmas series, based on the Hans Christian Andersen fairy tales, and the Mother's Day series, were begun in 1970.

All plates listed are made in porcelain in bas-relief and are hand-painted in "Copenhagen blue" using the true underglaze technique. Each plate is initialed on the back by its painter. Diameter: 7 inches. Foot rims pierced for hanging. Limited by year of issue. Edition size undisclosed. Not numbered. Artist's name appears on back.

Christmas Series

14-40-1.1
1970 *Hans Christian Andersen House.*
Artist: Gerhard Sausmark. Issue price: $14.50

14-40-1.2
1971 *The Little Match Girl.*
Artist: Mads Stage. Issue price: $15.00

14-40-1.3
1972 *Little Mermaid of Copenhagen.*
Rights from family of Edward Eriksen, sculptor. Issue price: $16.50

14-40-1.4
1973 *The Fir Tree.*
Artist: Svend Otto. Issue price: $22.00

14-40-1.5
1974 *The Chimney Sweep.*
Artist: Svend Otto. Issue price: $25.00

14-40-1.6
1975 *The Ugly Duckling.*
Artist: Svend Otto. Issue price: $27.50

14-40-1.7
1976 *The Snow Queen.*
Artist: Mads Stage. Issue price: $27.50

DENMARK
SVEND JENSEN

14-40-2.1

Mother's Day Series

14-40-2.1
1970 *A Bouquet for Mother.*
Artist: Maggi Baaring. Issue price: $14.50

14-40-2.2
1971 *Mother's Love.*
Artist: Nulle Oigaard. Issue price: $15.00

14-40-2.3
1972 *Good Night.*
Artist: Mads Stage. Issue price: $15.00

14-40-2.4
1973 *Flowers for Mother.*
Artist: Mads Stage. Issue price: $20.00

14-40-2.5
1974 *Daisies for Mother.*
Artist: Mads Stage. Issue price: $25.00

14-40-2.6
1975 *Surprise for Mother.*
Artist: Mads Stage. Issue price: $27.50

14-40-2.7
1976 *The Complete Gardener*
Artist: Mads Stage. Issue price: $27.50

14-69-1.1

ROYAL COPENHAGEN (Copenhagen)

DENMARK

The Royal Copenhagen Porcelain Manufactory, Denmark's oldest existing porcelain maker, was established by Franz Henrich Muller in 1775 with the support of the Queen Dowager, Juliane Marie. After years of experiment, Muller, a Danish chemist, and A. C. Luplau, a German modeller from Furstenberg, duplicated the secret method for true hard-paste porcelain. Royal Copenhagen has since manufactured dinnerware, vases, figurines, and limited-edition commemorative plates. Its trademark (three blue wavy lines and crown) symbolizes Denmark's three ancient waterways and the fact that the firm was at one time under royal control (1779-1867). The Danish blue underglaze technique was introduced in the 1880s by Arnold Krog, art director of Royal Copenhagen.

Royal Copenhagen has produced Christmas plates continuously since 1908. The firm issued small amounts of Christmas plates with text in English, German, French, and Czechoslovakian until 1944. The Mother's Day series began in 1971. To celebrate the company's own 200th anniversary, a new *Bicentennary* series was introduced in 1975 with yearly issues to commemorate other bicentennial anniversaries. The 1976 plate honors the American Bicentennial.

All plates listed are made in porcelain in bas-relief and are hand-painted in "Copenhagen blue" using the true underglaze technique. Each plate is initialed on the back by its painter. Foot rims pierced for hanging. Limited by year of issue. Edition size undisclosed. Not numbered. Artist's name has appeared on back of Christmas plates since 1955.

Christmas Series

Diameter: 7 inches (except 6 inches in 1908-1910 plates)

14-69-1.1
1908 *Madonna and Child.*
Artist: Chr. Thomsen. Issue price: $1.00

14-69-1.2
1909 *Danish Landscape.*
Artist: St. Ussing. Issue price: $1.00

14-69-1.3
1910 *The Magi.*
Artist: Chr. Thomsen. Issue price: $1.00

14-69-1.4
1911 *Danish Landscape.*
Artist: Oluf Jensen. Issue price: $1.00

14-69-1.5
1912 *Elderly Couple by Christmas Tree.*
Artist: Chr. Thomsen. Issue price: $1.00

14-69-1.6
1913 *Spire of Frederik's Church, Copenhagen.*
Artist: A. Boesen. Issue price: $1.50

14-69-1.7
1914 *Sparrows in Tree at Church of the Holy Spirit, Copenhagen.*
Artist: A. Boesen. Issue price: $1.50

14-69-1.8
1915 *Danish Landscape.*
Artist: A. Krog. Issue price: $1.50

DENMARK
ROYAL COPENHAGEN

14-69-1.9

14-69-1.9
1916 *Shepherd in the Field on Christmas Night.*
Artist: R. Bocher. Issue price: $1.50

14-69-1.10
1917 *Tower of Our Savior's Church, Copenhagen.*
Artist: Oluf Jensen. Issue price: $2.00

14-69-1.11
1918 *Sheep and Shepherds.*
Artist: Oluf Jensen. Issue price: $2.00

14-69-1.12
1919 *In the Park.*
Artist: Oluf Jensen. Issue price: $2.00

14-69-1.13
1920 *Mary with the Child Jesus.*
Artist: G. Rode. Issue price: $2.00

14-69-1.14
1921 *Aabenraa Marketplace.*
Artist: Oluf Jensen. Issue price: $2.00

14-69-1.15
1922 *Three Singing Angels.*
Artist: Mrs. Selschou-Olsen. Issue price: $2.00

14-69-1.16
1923 *Danish Landscape.*
Artist: Oluf Jensen. Issue price: $2.00

14-69-1.17
1924 *Christmas Star over the Sea and Sailing Ship.*
Artist: Benjamin Olsen. Issue price: $2.00

14-69-1.18
1925 *Street Scene from Christianshavn, Copenhagen.*
Artist: Oluf Jensen. Issue price: $2.00

14-69-1.19
1926 *View of Christianshavn Canal, Copenhagen.*
Artist: R. Bocher. Issue price: $2.00

14-69-1.20
1927 *Ship's Boy at the Tiller on Christmas Night.*
Artist: Benjamin Olsen. Issue price: $2.00

14-69-1.21

DENMARK
ROYAL COPENHAGEN

14-69-1.21
1928 *Vicar's Family on Way to Church.*
Artist: G. Rode. Issue price: $2.00

14-69-1.22
1929 *Grundtvig Church, Copenhagen.*
Artist: Oluf Jensen. Issue price: $2.00

14-69-1.23
1930 *Fishing Boats on the Way to the Harbor.*
Artist: Benjamin Olsen. Issue price: $2.50

14-69-1.24
1931 *Mother and Child.*
Artist: G. Rode. Issue price: $2.50

14-69-1.25
1932 *Frederiksberg Gardens with Statue of Frederik VI.*
Artist: Oluf Jensen. Issue price: $2.50

14-69-1.26
1933 *The Great Belt Ferry.*
Artist: Benjamin Olsen. Issue price: $2.50

14-69-1.27
1934 *The Hermitage Castle.*
Artist: Oluf Jensen. Issue price: $2.50

14-69-1.28
1935 *Fishing Boat off Kronborg Castle.*
Artist: Benjamin Olsen. Issue price: $2.50

14-69-1.29
1936 *Roskilde Cathedral.*
Artist: R. Bocher. Issue price: $2.50

14-69-1.30
1937 *Christmas Scene in Main Street, Copenhagen.*
Artist: Nils Thorsson. Issue price: $2.50

14-69-1.31
1938 *Round Church in Osterlars on Bornholm.*
Artist: Herne Nielsen. Issue price: $3.00

14-69-1.32
1939 *Expeditionary Ship in Pack-ice of Greenland.*
Artist: Sv. Nic. Nielsen. Issue price: $3.00

DENMARK
ROYAL COPENHAGEN

14-69-1.33

14-69-1.33
1940 *The Good Shepherd.*
Artist: Kai Lange. Issue price: $3.00

14-69-1.34
1941 *Danish Village Church.*
Artist: Th. Kjolner. Issue price: $3.00

14-69-1.35
1942 *Bell Tower of Old Church in Jutland.*
Artist: Nils Thorsson. Issue price: $4.00

14-69-1.36
1943 *Flight of Holy Family to Egypt.*
Artist: Nils Thorsson. Issue price: $4.00

14-69-1.37
1944 *Typical Danish Winter Scene.*
Artist: Viggo Olsen. Issue price: $4.00

14-69-1.38
1945 *A Peaceful Motif.*
Artist: R. Bocher. Issue price: $4.00

14-69-1.39
1946 *Zealand Village Church.*
Artist: Nils Thorsson. Issue price: $4.00

14-69-1.40
1947 *The Good Shepherd.*
Artist: Kai Lange. Issue price: $4.50

14-69-1.41
1948 *Nodebo Church at Christmastime.*
Artist: Th. Kjolner. Issue price: $4.50

14-69-1.42
1949 *Our Lady's Cathedral, Copenhagen.*
Artist: Hans H. Hansen. Issue price: $5.00

14-69-1.43
1950 *Boeslunde Church, Zealand.*
Artist: Viggo Olsen. Issue price: $5.00

14-69-1.44
1951 *Christmas Angel.*
Artist: R. Bocher. Issue price: $5.00

14-69-1.45

DENMARK
ROYAL COPENHAGEN

14-69-1.45
1952 *Christmas in the Forest.*
Artist: Kai Lange. Issue price: $5.00

14-69-1.46
1953 *Frederiksborg Castle.*
Artist: Th. Kjolner. Issue price: $6.00

14-69-1.47
1954 *Amalienborg Palace, Copenhagen.*
Artist: Kai Lange. Issue price: $6.00

14-69-1.48
1955 *Fano Girl.*
Artist: Kai Lange. Issue price: $7.00

14-69-1.49
1956 *Rosenborg Castle, Copenhagen.*
Artist: Kai Lange. Issue price: $7.00

14-69-1.50
1957 *The Good Shepherd.*
Artist: Hans H. Hansen. Issue price: $8.00

14-69-1.51
1958 *Sunshine over Greenland.*
Artist: Hans H. Hansen. Issue price: $9.00

14-69-1.52
1959 *Christmas Night.*
Artist: Hans H. Hansen. Issue price: $9.00

14-69-1.53
1960 *The Stag.*
Artist: Hans H. Hansen. Issue price: $10.00

14-69-1.54
1961 *Training Ship Danmark.*
Artist: Kai Lange. Issue price: $10.00

14-69-1.55
1962 *The Little Mermaid at Wintertime.*
Specific artist not named because of special
nature of this motif. Issue price: $11.00

14-69-1.56
1963 *Hojsager Mill.*
Artist: Kai Lange. Issue price: $11.00

DENMARK
ROYAL COPENHAGEN

14-69-1.57

14-69-1.57
1964 *Fetching the Christmas Tree.*
Artist: Kai Lange. Issue price: $11.00

14-69-1.58
1965 *Little Skaters.*
Artist: Kai Lange. Issue price: $12.00

14-69-1.59
1966 *Blackbird at Christmastime.*
Artist: Kai Lange. Issue price: $12.00

14-69-1.60
1967 *The Royal Oak.*
Artist: Kai Lange. Issue price: $13.00

14-69-1.61
1968 *The Last Umiak.*
Artist: Kai Lange. Issue price: $13.00

14-69-1.62
1969 *The Old Farmyard.*
Artist: Kai Lange. Issue price: $14.00

14-69-1.63
1970 *Christmas Rose and Cat.*
Artist: Kai Lange. Issue price: $14.00

14-69-1.64
1971 *Hare in Winter.*
Artist: Kai Lange. Issue price: $15.00

14-69-1.65
1972 *In the Desert.*
Artist: Kai Lange. Issue price: $16.00

14-69-1.66
1973 *Train Homeward Bound for Christmas.*
Artist: Kai Lange. Issue price: $22.00

14-69-1.67
1974 *Winter Twilight.*
Artist: Kai Lange. Issue price: $22.00

14-69-1.68
1975 *Queen's Palace.*
Artist: Kai Lange. Issue price: $27.50

14-69-1.69

DENMARK
ROYAL COPENHAGEN

14-69-1.69
1976 *Danish Watermill.*
Artist: Kai Lange. Issue price: $27.50

Mother's Day Series

Diameter: 6¼ inches

14-69-2.1
1971 *American Mother.*
Artist: Kamma Svensson. Issue price: $12.50

14-69-2.2
1972 *Oriental Mother.*
Artist: Kamma Svensson. Issue price: $14.00

14-69-2.3
1973 *Danish Mother.*
Artist: Arne Ungermann. Issue price: $16.00

14-69-2.4
1974 *Greenland Mother.*
Artist: Arne Ungermann. Issue price: $16.50

14-69-2.5
1975 *Bird in Nest.*
Artist: Arne Ungermann. Issue price: $20.00

14-69-2.6
1976 *Mermaids.*
Artist: Arne Ungermann. Issue price: $20.00

DENMARK
ROYAL COPENHAGEN

14-69-3.1

Bicentenary Series

Diameter: 7½ inches

14-69-3.1
1975 *Royal Copenhagen Bicentennial.*
Artist: Sven Vestergaard. Issue price: $30.00

14-69-3.2
1976 *United States Bicentennial.*
Artist: Sven Vestergaard. Issue price: $35.00

18-12-1.1
CRISTAL D'ALBRET (Vianne)

FRANCE

The Cristalleries et Verreries de Vianne was organized by Roger Witkind in 1918 for the manufacture of glass articles. The firm set aside a section of its facilities in 1967 for the production of collectors' lead crystal paperweights and plates to be issued under the name Cristal D'Albret. The *Four Seasons* series of limited-edition plates began in 1972 and was completed in 1974. The artist is Gilbert Poillerat.

All plates listed are made in full lead crystal with pressed designs. Not numbered, but with numbered certificate. Artist's initials etched on back of plate.

Four Seasons Series
Diameter: 8¼ inches.
Series of four plates.

18-12-1.1
1972 *Summer.*
Limited by announced edition size of 1,000.
Issue price: $64.00

18-12-1.2
1973 *Autumn.*
Limited by announced edition size of 648.
Issue price: $75.00

18-12-1.3
1973 *Spring.*
Limited by announced edition size of 312.
Issue price: $75.00

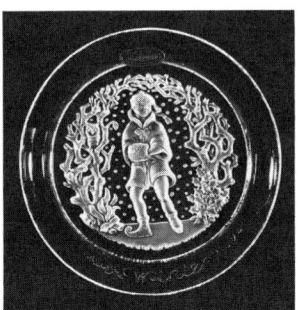

18-12-1.4
1974 *Winter.*
Edition size: undisclosed. Issue price: $88.00

Peace Plate
Diameter: 8¾ inches. Limited by announced edition size of 3,000.

18-12-2.1
1972 *Bird of Peace.*
Issue price: $64.00

FRANCE
D'ARCEAU-LIMOGES (Limoges)

18-15-1.1

Henri D'Arceau et Fils is one of the smaller houses in this famous porcelain center, and claims to adhere to the original "Grellet Standard" of 1768 for hand-craftsmanship. The firm was commissioned by the L'Esprit de Lafayette Society to produce the six-plate *Lafayette Legacy* series, 1973-1975, which chronicles the role of the Marquis de Lafayette in America's war for independence. The D'Arceau-Limoges Christmas series, begun in 1975, was inspired by the stained glass windows of the Cathedral at Chartres. The artist for both series is Andre Restieau. *Women of the Century*, the 12-plate series commissioned by the Chambre Syndicale de la Couture Parisienne, began in 1976. The series, with United Nations recognition, depicts western women's fashions from 1865 to 1965. The artist is Francois Ganeau.

All plates listed are made in porcelain. Back hanger attached. Limited by announced period of issue. Edition size undisclosed. Numbered with certificate. Artists' names appear on front of plate and initials on back.

Lafayette Legacy Series
Diameter: 8½ inches

18-15-1.1
1973 *The Secret Contract.*
Issue price: $12.00

18-15-1.2
1973 *The Landing at North Island.*
Issue price: $17.00

18-15-1.3
1974 *The Meeting at City Tavern.*
Issue price: $17.00

18-15-1.4
1974 *The Battle of Brandywine.*
Issue price: $17.00

18-15-1.5
1975 *The Messages to Franklin.*
Issue price: $17.00

18-15-1.6
1975 *The Siege at Yorktown.*
Issue price: $17.00

18-15-2.1

FRANCE
D'ARCEAU-LIMOGES

Christmas Series

Diameter: 8¼ inches

18-15-2.1
1975 *Flight into Egypt.*
Issue price: $24.32

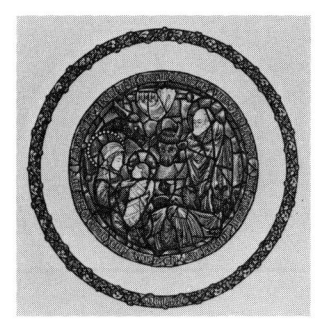

18-15-2.2
1976 *In the Cradle.*
Issue price: $24.32

"Women of the Century" Series

Diameter: 8½ inches

18-15-3.1
1976 *Scarlet en Crinoline.*
Issue price: $14.80

18-15-3.2
1976 *Sarah en Tournure.*
Issue price: $19.87

FRANCE
HAVILAND (Limoges)

18-30-1.1

In 1839, David Haviland of New York City became the first American importer of Limoges porcelain made from kaolin. When, in 1842, he found the French factories would not adjust methods to meet the tastes of his American market, Haviland established his own pottery in Limoges. In 1892, his son Theodore Haviland left the firm but remained in Limoges to set up Theodore Haviland & Co. for production of porcelain dinnerware and decorative pieces. In the 1930s, Theodore Haviland & Co. opened an American Haviland factory to produce domestic tableware; the firm also bought the original Haviland & Co. established by David Haviland. All Haviland collector's plates are produced in Limoges, France.

The twelve-plate Christmas series, begun in 1970, is based on the carol "The Twelve Days of Christmas". The five-plate Bicentennial series, introduced in 1972, commemorates events leading to the American Declaration of Independence. In 1973, the Mother's Day series of seven plates entitled *The French Collection* was started. The artist for all series is Remy Hetreau.

All plates listed are made in porcelain.

HAVILAND LIMOGES

Christmas Series

Diameter: 8-3/8 inches
Artist's signature appears on the back. Limited by announced edition size of 30,000.

18-30-1.1
1970 *A Partridge in a Pear Tree.*
Issue price: $25.00

18-30-1.2
1971 *Two Turtle Doves.*
Issue price: $25.00

18-30-1.3
1972 *Three French Hens.*
Issue price: $27.50

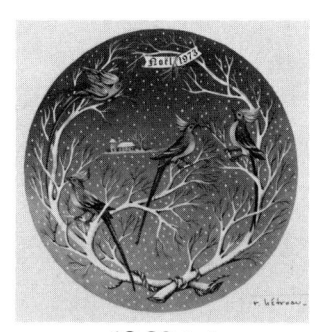

18-30-1.4
1973 *Four Colly Birds.*
Issue price: $28.50

18-30-1.5
1974 *Five Golden Rings.*
Issue price: $30.00

18-30-1.6
1975 *Six Geese A'Laying.*
Issue price: $32.50

18-30-1.7
1976 *Seven Swans A'Swimming.*
Issue price: $38.00

18-30-2.1

FRANCE
HAVILAND

Bicentennial Series

Diameter: 9¾ inches
Artist's signature appears on the back. Limited by announced edition size of 10,000.

18-30-2.1
1972 *Burning of the Gaspee.*
Issue price: $39.95

18-30-2.2
1973 *Boston Tea Party.*
Issue price: $39.95

18-30-2.3
1974 *First Continental Congress.*
Issue price: $39.95

18-30-2.4
1975 *Ride of Paul Revere.*
Issue price: $40.00

18-30-2.5
1976 *The Declaration of Independence.*
Issue price: $48.00

Mother's Day Series

Diameter: 8¼ inches
Numbered without certificate.
Artist's signature on front of plate.
Limited by edition size of 10,000.

18-30-3.1
1973 *Breakfast.*
Issue price: $29.95

18-30-3.2
1974 *The Wash.*
Issue price: $29.95

18-30-3.3
1975 *In the Park.*
Issue price: $30.00

18-30-3.4
1976 *To Market.*
Issue price: $38.00

FRANCE
HAVILAND PARLON (Limoges)

18-32-1.1

Haviland Parlon is a chapter in the intricate Haviland porcelain story. In 1853, Robert Haviland left New York City to work for his brother David Haviland in Limoges (see France, HAVILAND). In 1870, Robert's son, Charles Field Haviland, established a porcelain factory also in Limoges, using "Ch. Field Haviland" as his tradename. After he retired in 1881, the firm was known by several different names until 1942, when Robert Haviland (Robert's greatgrandson) purchased it. The firm is now known as Robert Haviland & C. Parlon.

The *Tapestry* series begun in 1971, reproduces six scenes from the French medieval tapestries "The Hunt of the Unicorn" now hanging in The Metropolitan Museum of Art, New York City. The Christmas series of famous Renaissance Madonnas began in 1972 and the Mother's Day series in 1975.

All plates listed are made in porcelain.

Tapestry Series

Diameter: 10 inches.
Not numbered. Limited by announced edition size of 10,000.

18-32-1.1
1971 *The Unicorn in Captivity.*
Issue price: $35.00

18-32-1.2
1972 *Start of the Hunt.*
Issue price: $35.00

18-32-1.3
1973 *Chase of the Unicorn.*
Issue price: $35.00

18-32-1.4
1974 *End of the Hunt.*
Issue price: $37.50

18-32-1.5
1975 *The Unicorn Surrounded.*
Issue price: $40.00

18-32-1.6
1976 *The Unicorn is Brought to the Castle.*
Issue price: $42.50

Christmas Series

Diameter: 10 inches.
Numbered, without certificate.
Limited by edition size of 5,000.

18-32-2.1
1972 *Madonna by Rafael.*
(Madonna della Saidia) Issue price: $35.00

18-32-2.2

FRANCE
HAVILAND PARLON

18-32-2.2
1973 *Madonnina by Feruzzi.*
(Madonna of the Streets) Issue price: $40.00

18-32-2.3
1974 *Madonna by Rafael.*
(The small Cowper Madonna)
Issue price: $42.50

18-32-2.4
1975 *Madonna by Murillo.*
Issue price: $42.50

Mother's Day Series

Diameter: 7¾ inches.
Not numbered. Limited by
announced edition size of 15,000.

18-32-3.1
1975 *Mother and Child.*
Artist: Marion Carlsen. Issue price: $37.50

18-32-3.2
1976 *Pinky and Baby.*
Artist: Marian Carlsen. Issue price: $42.50

FRANCE
LALIQUE (undisclosed, Alsace)

18-46-1.1

Rene Lalique began his career as a jeweler producing many designs in the Art Nouveau style. In 1902, his interest turned to glass-making and he acquired a small glassworks at Clairfontaine. In 1909, Lalique opened a glassworks at Combs, and in 1918 he constructed the present factory in Alsace. Here, Lalique began to produce glass items in the Art Deco style. His designs, usually created in pressed lead crystal, are noted for the frosted and satin effects of the glass. Until his death in 1945, Lalique produced numerous commercial glass objects such as perfume bottles, vases, and figurines. In 1965, Lalique & Cie. began a series of annual crystal plates designed by Marie-Claude Lalique, Rene's granddaughter. The subjects are flowers and animals.

All plates listed are made in transparent full lead crystal with etched designs. Diameter: 8½ inches. Limited by announced edition size which has gradually increased from 5,000 in 1966 to 8,000 in 1975. Not numbered. Etched "Lalique-France" on back of plate.

Annual Series

18-46-1.1
1965 *Deux Oiseaux.*
Limited by announced edition size of 2,000.
Issue price: $25.00

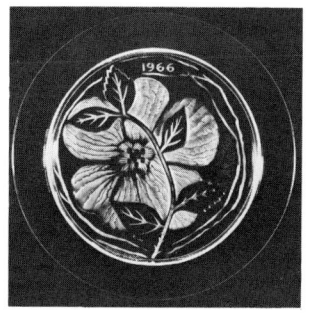

18-46-1.2
1966 *Dreamrose.*
Limited by announced edition size of 5,000.
Issue price: $25.00

18-46-1.3
1967 *Fish Ballet.*
Issue price: $25.00

18-46-1.4
1968 *Gazelle Fantasie.*
Issue price: $25.00

18-46-1.5
1969 *Papillon.*
Issue price: $30.00

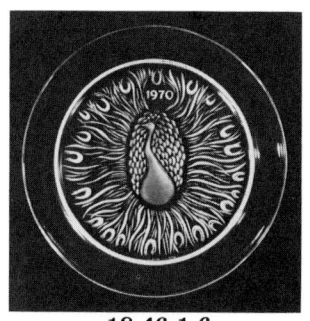

18-46-1.6
1970 *Peacock.*
Issue price: $30.00

18-46-1.7
1971 *Hibou.*
Issue price: $35.00

18-46-1.8
1972 *Coquillage.*
Issue price: $40.00

18-46-1.9

FRANCE
LALIQUE

18-46-1.9
1973 *Jayling.*
Issue price: $42.50

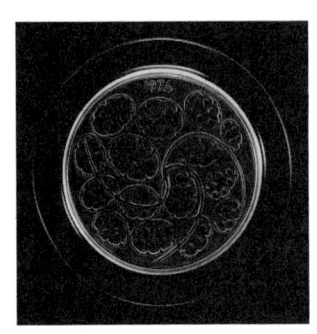

18-46-1.10
1974 *Silver Pennies.*
Issue price: $47.50

18-46-1.11
1975 *Fish Duet.*
Limited by announced edition size of 8,000.
Issue price: $50.00

18-46-1.12
1976 *Eagle.*
Issue price: $60.00

FRANCE
ROYAL LIMOGES (Limoges)

18-69-1.1

Royal Limoges porcelain is produced in three factories, among them the Ancienne Manufacture Royale, the oldest existing French factory manufacturing hard-paste porcelain. The firm's limited-edition collector's plates were produced by the A. Lanternier & Cie. factory established in 1798. The inspiration for Royal Limoges' two Christmas plates was the centuries-old Provencal custom of modeling tiny clay statues entitled "Les Santons de Noel" (The Little Saints of Christmas) to put into creches. The artist is Roch Popelier.

All plates listed are made in porcelain. Diameter: 8¾ inches. Limited by edition size of 5,000. Numbered without certificate. Artist's name appears on back.

Christmas Series

18-69-1.1
1972 *The Nativity.*
Issue price: $25.00

18-69-1.2
1973 *The Three Wise Men.*
Issue price: $27.50

22-6-1.1
BAREUTHER (Waldsassen)

GERMANY

The Bareuther & Co. porcelain factory began to produce dinnerware, vases, and giftware in 1867. The small shop was established with a porcelain kiln and an annular brick kiln by sculptor Johann Mattaeus Ries. In 1884, Ries' son sold the shop to Oakar Bareuther who continued to produce fine tableware.

The company observed the factory's 100th anniversary with a series of limited-edition Christmas plates introduced in 1967. Bareuther's Mother's Day series, begun in 1969, is from original drawings by Ludwig Richter (1803-1884). The Father's Day series of the great castles of Germany, drawn by Hans Mueller, began in 1969. The Thanksgiving series started in 1971 and is of American Thanksgiving scenes. The artist is Kurt C. Beilefeld.

All plates listed are made in porcelain decorated in cobalt blue underglaze. Diameter: 8 inches. Foot rims pierced for hanging. Not numbered.

Christmas Series

Limited by announced edition size of 10,000. The artist for all plates except 1971 is Hans Mueller.

22-6-1.1
1967 *Stiftskirche.*
Issue price: $12.00

22-6-1.2
1968 *Kappl.*
Issue price: $12.00

22-6-1.3
1969 *Christkindlesmarkt.*
Issue price: $12.00

22-6-1.4
1970 *Chapel in Oberndorf.*
Issue price: $12.00

22-6-1.5
1971 *Toys for Sale.*
From drawing by Ludwig Richter (1803-1884).
Issue price: $13.50

22-6-1.6
1972 *Christmas in Munich.*
Issue price: $15.00

22-6-1.7
1973 *Christmas Sleigh Ride.*
Issue price: $15.00

22-6-1.8
1974 *Church in the Black Forest.*
Issue price: $19.00

GERMANY
BAREUTHER

22-6-1.9

22-6-1.9
1975 *Snowman.*
Issue price: $21.50

22-6-1.10
1976 *Chapel in the Hills.*
Issue price: $23.50

Father's Day Series

Limited by announced edition size of 2,500.

22-6-2.1
1969 *Castle Neuschwanstein.*
Issue price: $12.00

22-6-2.2
1970 *Castle Pfalz.*
Issue price: $12.00

22-6-2.3
1971 *Castle Heidelberg.*
Issue price: $13.50

22-6-2.4
1972 *Castle Hohenschwangau.*
Issue price: $15.00

22-6-2.5
1973 *Castle Katz.*
Issue price: $15.00

22-6-2.6
1974 *Wurzburg Castle.*
Issue price: $19.00

22-6-2.7
1975 *Castle Lichtenstein.*
Issue price: $21.50

22-6-2.8
1976 *Castle Hohenzollern.*
Issue price: $23.00

22-6-3.1

GERMANY
BAREUTHER

Mother's Day Series

Limited by announced edition size of 5,000.

22-6-3.1
1969 *Mother and Children.*
Issue price: $12.00

22-6-3.2
1970 *Mother and Children.*
Issue price: $12.00

22-6-3.3
1971 *Mother and Children.*
Issue price: $13.50

22-6-3.4
1972 *Mother and Children.*
Issue price: $15.00

22-6-3.5
1973 *Mother and Children.*
Issue price: $15.00

22-6-3.6
1974 *Musical Children.*
Issue price: $19.00

22-6-3.7
1975 *Spring Outing.*
Issue price: $21.50

22-6-3.8
1976 *Rocking the Cradle.*
Issue price: $23.00

GERMANY
BAREUTHER

22-6-4.1

Thanksgiving Series

Limited by announced edition size of 2,500.

22-6-4.1
1971 *First Thanksgiving.*
Issue price: $13.50

22-6-4.2
1972 *Harvest.*
Issue price: $15.00

22-6-4.3
1973 *Country Road in Autumn.*
Issue price: $15.00

22-6-4.4
1974 *Old Mill.*
Issue price: $19.00

22-6-4.5
1975 *Wild Deer in Forest.*
Issue price: $21.50

22-6-4.6
1976 *Thanksgiving on the Farm.*
Issue price: $23.50

22-8-1.1
BERLIN DESIGN (Staffelstein)

GERMANY

Berlin Design's limited-edition plates, mugs, and other collectibles are manufactured by the Kaiser Porcelain Co. (see Germany, KAISER). The Christmas series, introduced in 1970, is of Yule festivities in German towns. The Mother's Day series of animal mothers and their young began in 1971. The Father's Day series, also begun 1971, depicts episodes in American history. Names of artists undisclosed.

All plates listed are made in porcelain decorated in cobalt blue underglaze. Limited by year of issue and by edition size where announced. Foot rims pierced for hanging.

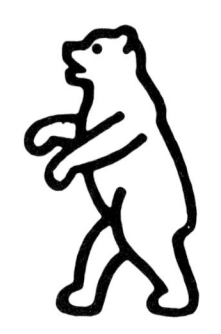

Christmas Series
Diameter: 7-5/8 inches.

22-8-1.1
1970 *Christmas in Bernkastel.*
Limited by announced edition size of 4,000.
Issue price: $14.50

22-8-1.2
1971 *Christmas in Rothenburg on Tauber.*
Limited by announced edition size of 20,000.
Issue price: $14.50

22-8-1.3
1972 *Christmas in Michelstadt.*
Issue price: $15.00

22-8-1.4
1973 *Christmas in Wendelstein.*
Issue price: $20.00

22-8-1.5
1974 *Christmas in Bremen.*
Issue price: $25.00

22-8-1.6
1975 *Christmas in Dortland.*
Issue price: $30.00

22-8-1.7
1976 *Christmas Eve in Augsburg.*
Issue price: $32.00

GERMANY
BERLIN

22-8-2.1

Father's Day Series

Diameter: 8 inches.

22-8-2.1
1971 *Brooklyn Bridge on Opening Day.*
Limited by announced edition size of 12,000.
Issue price: $14.50

22-8-2.2
1972 *The Continent Spanned.*
Limited by announced edition size of 3,000.
Issue price: $15.00

22-8-2.3
1973 *The Landing of Columbus.*
Limited by announced edition size of 2,000.
Issue price: $18.00

22-8-2.4
1974 *Balloon.*
Issue price: $25.00

22-8-2.5
1975 *Washington Crossing the Delaware.*
Issue price: $30.00

22-8-2.6
1976 *Tom Thumb.*
Issue price: $32.00

22-8-3.1

GERMANY
BERLIN

Mother's Day Series

Diameter: 7-5/8 inches.

22-8-3.1
1971 *Grey Poodles.*
Limited by announced edition size of 20,000.
Issue price: $14.50

22-8-3.2
1972 *Fledglings.*
Limited by announced edition size of 10,000.
Issue size: $15.00

22-8-3.3
1973 *Duck Family.*
Limited by announced edition size of 5,000.
Issue price: $16.50

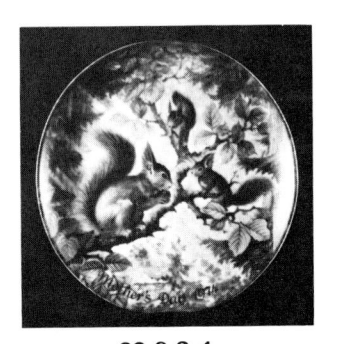

22-8-3.4
1974 *Squirrels.*
Issue price: $22.50

22-8-3.5
1975 *Cats.*
Issue price: $30.00

22-8-3.6
1976 *A Doe and her Fawn.*
Issue price: $32.00

GERMANY
DANISH CHURCH (Waldsassen)

22-13-1.1

Danish Church plates, formerly called Roskild Church plates, are produced by a division of Bareuther & Co. (see Germany, BAREUTHER). The *Church* series is of famous Danish churches. Name of artist undisclosed.

All plates listed are made in porcelain decorated in cobalt blue underglaze. Diameter: 7¾ inches. Foot rims pierced for hanging. Limited by year of issue. Edition size undisclosed. Not numbered.

Kirke Platten

Church Series

22-13-1.1
1968 *Roskilde Cathedral.*
Issue price: $12.00

22-13-1.2
1969 *Ribe Cathedral.*
Issue price: $13.00

22-13-1.3
1970 *Marmor Kirken.*
Issue price: $13.00

22-13-1.4
1971 *Ejby Kirken.*
Issue price: $13.00

22-13-1.5
1972 *Kalundborg Kirken.*
Issue price: $13.00

22-13-1.6
1973 *Grundtvig Kirken.*
Issue price: $15.00

22-13-1.7
1974 *Broager Kirken.*
Issue price: $15.00

22-13-1.8
1975 *Sct. Knuds Kirken.*
Issue price: $18.00

22-15-1.1
DRESDEN (Hoxter)

GERMANY

The Dresden-Meissen area of Germany is rich in kaolin essential for fine porcelain. It was in this region in 1708, that alchemist Johann Friedrich Bottger duplicated the secret of Chinese porcelain and produced the first hard-paste porcelain in the Western world. Presently, "Dresden" china has no geographic connotation. Plates with the Dresden trademark are produced by the Furstenberg factory (see Germany, FURSTENBERG). Dresden introduced its Christmas plate series in 1971 and its Mother's Day series in 1972. The artist for both series is Hans Waldheimer.

All plates listed are made in porcelain with cobalt blue underglaze center, white baroque rim, and hand-polished matte gold edge. Diameter: 7½ inches. Back hanger attached. Not Numbered.

Christmas Series

Limited by announced edition size of 3,500.

22-15-1.1
1971 *Shepherd Scene.*
Issue price: $14.50

22-15-1.2
1972 *Niklas Church.*
Issue price: $18.00

22-15-1.3
1973 *Schwanstein Church.*
Issue price: $18.00

22-15-1.4
1974 *Village Scene.*
Issue price: $20.00

22-15-1.5
1975 *Rothenberg Scene.*
Issue price: $24.00

22-15-1.6
1976 *Not available at presstime.*
Limited by announced edition size of 5,000.
Issue price: $26.00

GERMANY
DRESDEN

22-15-2.1

Mother's Day Series

Limited by announced edition size of 8,000.

22-15-2.1
1972 *Doe and Fawns.*
Issue price: $15.00

22-15-2.2
1973 *Mare and Colt.*
Issue price: $16.00

22-15-2.3
1974 *Tiger and Cub.*
Issue price: $20.00

22-15-2.4
1975 *Dachshund Family.*
Issue price: $24.00

22-15-2.5
1976 *Mother Owl and Young.*
Limited by announced edition size of 5,000.
Issue price: $26.00

22-23-1.1
FURSTENBERG (Hoxter)

GERMANY

Furstenberg, West Germany's oldest surviving porcelain factory, was established in 1747 in the castle of Furstenberg by order of Duke Karl I of Brunswick. He decreed that each piece of porcelain be initialed with a blue "F" which was later surmounted by a crown. The factory, privately owned since 1859, produces tableware, vases, and other decorative accessories, as well as figurines and plaques.

The Christmas series and Easter series were introduced in 1971. The Mother's Day series began in 1972. These plates are made in porcelain decorated in cobalt blue underglaze. Diameter: 7½ inches. Back hanger attached. Not Numbered.

A second *Deluxe* Christmas plate series, by artist Eva Grossberg, began in 1971 and ended in 1973. These plates are made in porcelain decorated in various colors with cobalt blue border and hand-decoration in 18k gold. Diameter: 9½ inches. Numbered without certificate.

Christmas Series
Diameter: 7½ inches.
Artist: Walter Schoen.

22-23-1.1
1971 *Rabbits.*
Limited by announced edition size of 8,500.
Issue price: $15.00

22-23-1.2
1972 *Snowy Village.*
Limited by announced edition size of 6,000.
Issue price: $15.00

22-23-1.3
1973 *Christmas Eve.*
Limited by announced edition size of 5,000.
Issue price: $18.00

22-23-1.4
1974 *Sparrows.*
Limited by announced edition size of 4,000.
Issue price: $20.00

22-23-1.5
1975 *Deer Family.*
Limited by announced edition size of 4,000.
Issue price: $24.00

22-23-1.6
1976 *Winter Birds Feeding from Pine Cones.*
Artist: I. Gahries. Limited by announced edition size of 4,000. Issue price: $25.00

GERMANY
FURSTENBERG

22-23-2.1

Deluxe Christmas Series

Diameter: 9½ inches. Artists signature appears on back of plate.

22-23-2.1
1971 *Three Wise Men.*
Limited by edition size of 1,500.
Issue price: $45.00

22-23-2.2
1972 *Holy Family and Angel.*
Limited by edition size of 2,000.
Issue price: $45.00

22-23-2.3
1973 *Christmas Eve.*
Limited by edition size of 2,000.
Issue price: $60.00

Easter Series

Diameter: 7½ inches.

22-23-3.1
1971 *Sheep.*
Limited by announced edition size of 3,000.
Issue price: $15.00

22-23-3.2
1972 *Chicks.*
Limited by announced edition size of 6,000.
Issue price: $15.00

22-23-3.3
1973 *Rabbits.*
Limited by announced edition size of 4,000.
Issue price: $16.00

22-23-3.4
1974 *Pussy Willows.*
Limited by announced edition size of 4,000.
Issue price: $20.00

22-23-3.5
1975 *Easter Window.*
Limited by announced edition size of 4,000.
Issue price: $24.00

22-23-3.6
1976 *Gathering Easter Flowers.*
Artist: I. Gahries. Limited by announced edition size of 4,000. Issue price: $25.00

22-23-4.1

GERMANY
FURSTENBERG

Mother's Day Series

Diameter: 7½ inches.

22-23-4.1
1972 *Hummingbird.*
Limited by announced edition size of 7,500.
Issue price: $15.00

22-23-4.2
1973 *Hedgehogs.*
Limited by announced edition size of 5,000.
Issue price: $16.00

22-23-4.3
1974 *Doe with Fawn.*
Limited by announced edition size of 4,000.
Issue price: $20.00

22-23-4.4
1975 *Swan Family.*
Limited by announced edition size of 4,000.
Issue price: $24.00

22-23-4.5
1976 *Koala Bear and Young.*
Artist: I. Gahries. Limited by announced edition size of 4,000. Issue price: $25.00

GERMANY
GOEBEL (Oeslau)

22-27-1.1

W. Goebel Co. was established in 1871 in Oeslau by Franz Detlev Goebel and his son William. They began business by producing porcelain tableware. After the turn of the century the firm added porcelain and earthenware figurines plus other gift articles. In 1934, Goebel was the first to produce figurines based on the original drawings of children by Berta Hummel, who in that year became Sister Maria Innocentia Hummel at the Franciscan convent in Siessen. All Goebel collector's plates are distributed in the United States by Hummelwerk, a subsidiary of Goebel. To celebrate the 100th anniversary of its porcelain factory in Oeslau, Goebel began a series in 1971 of annual limited-edition plates with the M. I. Hummel designs.

The *Hummel* Anniversary series began in 1975 with a new plate to be issued every five years. Other Goebel plate series are the *Wildlife* series from 1974, and a Mother's series started in 1975.

All plates listed are made in porcelain in bas-relief and are hand-painted. Foot rims pierced for hanging. Limited by year of issue. Edition size undisclosed. Not numbered.

Hummel Annual Series

Diameter: 7½ inches.
Hummel signature appears on front.

22-27-1.1
1971 *Heavenly Angel.*
Issue price: $25.00

22-27-1.2
1972 *Hear Ye, Hear Ye.*
Issue price: $30.00

22-27-1.3
1973 *Globe Trotter.*
Issue price: $32.50

22-27-1.4
1974 *Goose Girl.*
Issue price: $40.00

22-27-1.5
1975 *Ride into Christmas.*
Issue price: $50.00

22-27-1.6
1976 *Apple Tree Girl.*
Issue price: $50.00

22-27-2.1

GERMANY
GOEBEL

Wildlife Series

Diameter: 7½ inches.
Name of artist undisclosed.

22-27-2.1
1974 *Robin.*
Issue price: $45.00

22-27-2.2
1975 *Blue Titmouse.*
Issue price: $50.00

22-27-2.3
1976 *Barn Owl.*
Issue price: $50.00

Hummel Anniversary Series

Diameter: 10 inches.
Hummel signature appears on front.

22-27-3.1
1975 *Stormy Weather.*
Issue price: $100.00

GERMANY
GOEBEL

22-27-4.1

Mother's Series
Diameter: 7½ inches.
Artist: Gerhard Bochmann

22-27-4.1
1975 *Rabbits.*
Issue price: $45.00

22-27-4.2
1976 *Cats.*
Issue price: $45.00

22-42-1.1
KAISER (Staffelstein)

GERMANY

Kaiser Porcelain Company's history began in 1872 when the porcelain painter August Alboth set up his own workshop in Colburg. In 1899, his son Ernst moved the business to Bavaria. Marriage brought the Alboth and Kaiser families together in 1922 resulting in the ALKA trademark; the first two letters from both names. The present trademark is AK surmounted by a crown. In 1938, the company purchased the old Bavarian firm, Silbermann Bros., which had been awarded a royal diploma in 1882 for its "magnificent" use of cobalt blue underglaze. Kaiser opened its modern factory in Staffelstein in 1953. Long a producer of porcelain dinner and coffee sets and figurines, Kaiser introduced its first limited-edition plates, the Christmas series, in 1970. The Mother's Day series started in 1971. To observe the company's own centennial, The *Anniversary* series began in 1972.

All plates listed are made in porcelain decorated in cobalt blue underglaze. Diameter: 7½ inches. Foot rims pierced for hanging. Limited by year of issue and by edition size where announced. Not numbered.

Christmas Series

Foot rims pierced for hanging.

22-42-1.1
1970 *Waiting for Santa Claus.*
Artist: Toni Schoener. Issue price: $12.50

22-42-1.2
1971 *Silent Night.*
Artist: Kurt Bauer. Issue price: $13.50

22-42-1.3
1972 *Welcome Home.*
Artist: Kurt Bauer. Issue price: $16.50

22-42-1.4
1973 *Holy Night.*
Artist: Toni Schoener. Issue price: $18.00

22-42-1.5
1974 *Christmas Carolers.*
Artist: Kurt Bauer. Limited by announced edition size of 8,000. Issue price: $25.00

22-42-1.6
1975 *Bringing Home the Christmas Tree.*
Artist: Joann Northcott. Issue price: $25.00

22-42-1.7
1976 *Christ the Saviour is Born.*
Artist: Cark Maratta. Issue price: $25.00

GERMANY
KAISER

22-42-2.1

Mother's Day Series
Artist: Toni Schoener

22-42-2.1
1971 *Mare and Foal.*
Issue Price: $13.00

22-42-2.2
1972 *Flowers for Mother.*
Issue price: $16.50

22-42-2.3
1973 *Cats.*
Issue price: $17.00

22-42-2.4
1974 *Fox.*
Limited by announced edition size of 7,000.
Issue price: $22.00

22-42-2.5
1975 *German Shepherd.*
Issue price: $25.00

22-42-2.6
1976 *Swan and Cygnets.*
Issue price: $25.00

22-42-3.1　　　　　　　　　　　　　　　　　　　　　　　　　　　　　　　　　　　**GERMANY**
　　KAISER

Anniversary Series

Artist: Toni Schoener

22-42-3.1
1972 *Love Birds.*
Issue price: $16.50

22-42-3.2
1973 *In the Park.*
Issue price: $18.00

22-42-3.3
1974 *Canoeing down River.*
Limited by announced edition size of 7,000.
Issue price: $22.00

22-42-3.4
1975 *Tender Moment.*
Limited by announced edition size of 7,000.
Issue price: $25.00

22-42-3.5
1976 *Serenade for Lovers.*
Issue price: $25.00

GERMANY
LIHS LINDNER (Kueps)

22-47-1.1

The Lindner porcelain factory was established by Ernst Lindner in the 1930s in Kueps, Bavaria. Collector's plates by Lihs Lindner are the product of collaboration between Lindner and Helmut H. Lihs of Long Beach, California. Lihs provides motifs and sketches which are finished by Lindner's artist, Josef Neubauer. Lindner also produces bells, vases, and various porcelain items. The Christmas and Mother's Day plate series were both started in 1972. The Easter series began in 1973.

All plates listed are made in cobalt porcelain and decorated with 24k gold. Diameter: 7½ inches. Foot rims pierced for hanging. Numbered without certificate.

Christmas Series
Limited by edition size of 6,000.

22-47-1.1
1972 *Little Drummer Boy.*
Issue price: $25.00

22-47-1.2
1973 *The Little Carolers.*
Issue price: $25.00

22-47-1.3
1974 *Peace on Earth.*
Issue price: $25.00

22-47-1.4
1975 *Christmas Cheer.*
Issue price: $30.00

22-47-1.5
1976 *The Joy of Christmas.*
Issue price: $30.00

Mother's Day Series

22-47-2.1
1972 *Mother and Child.*
Limited by edition size of 1,000.
Issue price: $25.00

22-47-2.2

GERMANY
LIHS LINDNER

22-47-2.2
1973 *Mother and Child.*
Limited by edition size of 2,000.
Issue price: $25.00

22-47-2.3
1974 *A Bouquet for Mother.*
Limited by edition size of 2,000.
Issue price: $25.00

22-47-2.4
1975 *We Wish You Happiness, Mother.*
Limited by edition size of 2,000.
Issue price: $28.00

Easter Series

Limited by edition size of 1,500.

22-47-3.1
1973 *Happy Easter.*
Issue price: $25.00

22-47-3.2
1974 *Spring-time.*
Issue price: $25.00

22-47-3.3
1975 *With Love to You at Easter.*
Issue price: $28.00

GERMANY
ROSENTHAL (Selb, Selb-Plossberg, Munchen, Kronach, Bad Soden)

22-69-1.1

In 1879, Philip Rosenthal Sr. began business in Germany by purchasing porcelain from the Heutschenheuter porcelain factory and painting it with his own designs. In 1895, Rosenthal established a porcelain factory of his own in Kronach. His porcelain was signed with the name "Rosenthal" at a time when other manufacturers were using only symbols to mark their ware. Philip Rosenthal became head of the firm in 1937.

Rosenthal's *Traditional* Christmas series began in 1910. Between 1969 and 1971 Rosenthal reissued small quantities (no more than 500 per reissue) of some of these plates (1910-1971). Reissued plates have a modern (post-1957) backstamp regardless of year of plate depicted and their foot rims are not pierced. In 1971, Rosenthal discontinued reissuing any previous years' collector's plates and therefore the *Traditional* Christmas series now qualify as limited-editions. All Rosenthal collector's plates are now produced only during their current year.

The Rosenthal *Wiinblad* Christmas series of intricate modern designs began in 1971. These plates, with an 18k gold rim and partial hand-painting in 18 colors, are by artist Bjorn Wiinblad. The Rosenthal *Trester* series began in 1975 with artwork by Lorraine Trester. The *Oriental Nights* series depicting oriental musicians began in 1976 with artwork by Bjorn Wiinblad.

All plates listed are made in porcelain. Foot rims pierced for hanging before 1971, thereafter back hanger attached. Not numbered.

Traditional Christmas Series

Diameter: 8½ inches. Artists' name appears on back of plate.

22-69-1.1
1910 *Winter Peace.*
Artist: Jul V. Guldrandson

22-69-1.2
1911 *The Three Wise Men.*
Artist: Heinrich Vogoler

22-69-1.3
1912 *Stardust.*
Artist: Paul Rieth

22-69-1.4
1913 *Christmas Lights.*
Artist: Julius Dietz

22-69-1.5
1914 *Christmas Song.*
Artist: Prof. L. V. Zumbusch

22-69-1.6
1915 *Walking to Church.*
Artist: Jul V. Guldbrandson

22-69-1.7
1916 *Christmas During War.*
Artist: Jul V. Guldbrandson

22-69-1.8
1917 *Angel of Peace.*
Artist: Moere

22-69-1.9

GERMANY
ROSENTHAL

22-69-1.9
1918 *Peace on Earth.*
Artist: Pfeiffer

22-69-1.10
1919 *St. Christopher with the Christ Child.*
Artist: Dr. W. Schertel

22-69-1.11
1920 *The Manger in Bethlehem.*
Artist: Dr. W. Schertel

22-69-1.12
1921 *Christmas in the Mountains.*
Artist: Jupp Wiertz

22-69-1.13
1922 *Advent Branch.*
Artist: F. Nicolai

22-69-1.14
1923 *Children in the Winter Wood.*
Artist: Ernst Hofer

22-69-1.15
1924 *Deers in the Woods.*
Artist: Theo Karner

22-69-1.16
1925 *The Three Wise Men.*
Artist: Tauschek

22-69-1.17
1926 *Christmas in the Mountains.*
Artist: Theo Schmutz-Baudess

22-69-1.18
1927 *Station on the Way.*
Artist: Theo Schmutz-Baudess

22-69-1.19
1928 *Chalet Christmas.*
Artist: Heinrich Fink

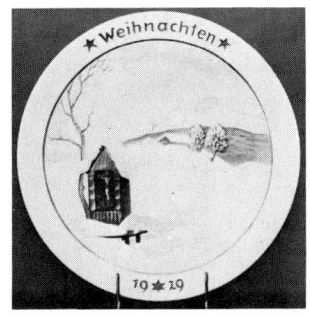

22-69-1.20
1929 *Christmas in the Alps.*
Artist: Heinrich Fink.

GERMANY
ROSENTHAL

22-69-1.21

22-69-1.21
1930 *Group of Deer Under the Pines.*
Artist: Theo Karner.

22-69-1.22
1931 *Path of the Magi.*
Artist: Heinrich Fink

22-69-1.23
1932 *Christ Child.*
Artist: Otto Koch

22-69-1.24
1933 *Thru the Night to Light.*
Artist: Hans Schiffner

22-69-1.25
1934 *Christmas Peace.*
Artist: Heinrich Fink

22-69-1.26
1935 *Christmas by the Sea.*
Artist: Heinrich Fink

22-69-1.27
1936 *Nurnberg Angel.*
Artist: Heinrich Fink

22-69-1.28
1937 *Berchtesgaden.*
Artist: Heinrich Fink

22-69-1.29
1938 *Christmas in the Alps.*
Artist: Heinrich Fink

22-69-1.30
1939 *Schneekoppe Mountain.*
Artist: Heinrich Fink

22-69-1.31
1940 *Marien Church in Danzig.*
Artist: Walter Mutze

22-69-1.32
1941 *Strassburg Cathedral.*
Artist: Walter Mutze

22-69-1.33

GERMANY
ROSENTHAL

22-69-1.33
1942 *Marianburg Castle.*
Artist: Walter Mutze.

22-69-1.34
1943 *Winter Idyll.*
Artist: Amadeus Dier.

22-69-1.35
1944 *Wood Scape.*
Artist: Willi Hein.

22-69-1.36
1945 *Christmas Peace.*
Artist: Aldred Mundel.

22-69-1.37
1946 *Christmas in an Alpine Valley.*
Artist: Willi Hein.

22-69-1.38
1947 *The Dillingen Madonna.*
Artist: Louis Hagen. (c. 15th Century)

22-69-1.39
1948 *Message to the Shepherds.*
Artist: Richard Hoffman.

22-69-1.40
1949 *The Holy Family.*
Artist: Prof. Karl.

22-69-1.41
1950 *Christmas in the Forest.*
Artist: Willi Hein.

22-69-1.42
1951 *Star of Bethlehem.*
Artist: Anne V. Groote.

22-69-1.43
1952 *Christmas in the Alps.*
Artist: Willi Hein.

22-69-1.44
1953 *The Holy Light.*
Artist: Willi Hein.

GERMANY
ROSENTHAL

22-69-1.45

22-69-1.45
1954 *Christmas Eve.*
Artist: Willi Hein.

22-69-1.46
1955 *Christmas in a Village.*
Artist: Willi Hein.

22-69-1.47
1956 *Christmas in the Alps.*
Artist: Willi Hein.

22-69-1.48
1957 *Christmas by the Sea.*
Artist: Willi Hein.

22-69-1.49
1958 *Christmas Eve.*
Artist: Willi Hein.

22-69-1.50
1959 *Midnight Mass.*
Artist: Willi Hein.

22-69-1.51
1960 *Christmas in a Small Village.*
Artist: Willi Hein.

22-69-1.52
1961 *Solitary Christmas.*
Artist: Willi Hein.

22-69-1.53
1962 *Christmas Eve.*
Artist: Willi Hein.

22-69-1.54
1963 *Silent Night.*
Artist: Willi Hein.

22-69-1.55
1964 *Christmas Market in Nurnberg.*
Artist: Georg Kuspert.

22-69-1.56
1965 *Christmas Munich.*
Artist: Georg Kuspert.

22-69-1.57

GERMANY
ROSENTHAL

22-69-1.57
1966 *Christmas in Ulm.*
Artist: Georg Kuspert.

22-69-1.58
1967 *Christmas in Reginburg.*
Artist: Georg Kuspert.

22-69-1.59
1968 *Christmas in Bremen.*
Artist: Georg Kuspert.

22-69-1.60
1969 *Christmas in Rothenburg.*
Artist: Georg Kuspert.

22-69-1.61
1970 *Christmas in Cologne.*
Artist: Georg Kuspert.

22-69-1.62
1971 *Christmas in Garmisch.*
Artist: Georg Kuspert. Issue price: $66.00

22-69-1.63
1972 *Christmas Celebration in Francone.*
Artist: Georg Kuspert. Issue price: $66.00

22-69-1.64
1973 *Christmas in Lubeck-Holstein.*
Artist: Georg Kuspert. Issue price: $84.00

22-69-1.65
1974 *Christmas in Wurzburg.*
Artist: Georg Kuspert. Issue price: $85.00

22-69-1.66
1975 *Freiburg Cathedral.*
Artist: Helmut Drexler. Issue price: $75.00

22-69-1.67
1976 *The Castle of Cochen.*
Artist: Helmut Drexler. Issue price: $95.00

GERMANY
ROSENTHAL

22-69-2.1

Wiinblad
Christmas Series

Diameter: 11½ inches. Artist's signature appears on front of plate.

22-69-2.1
1971 *Madonna and Child.*
Limited by announced edition size of 8,000.
Issue price: $100.00

22-69-2.2
1972 *King Caspar.*
Issue price: $100.00

22-69-2.3
1973 *King Melchior.*
Issue price: $125.00

22-69-2.4
1974 *King Balthazar.*
Issue price: $125.00

22-69-2.5
1975 *The Ascension.*
Issue price: $195.00

22-69-2.6
1976 *Angel with Trumpet.*
Issue price: $195.00

22-69-3.1

GERMANY
ROSENTHAL

Lorraine Trester Series

Diameter: 9-7/8 inches. Artist's signature appears on front of plate.

22-69-3.1
1975 *Once Upon a Summertime.*
Limited by edition size of 5,000.
Issue price: $60.00

Oriental Nights Series

Diameter: 6½ inches. Edition size undisclosed. Not numbered.

22-69-4.1
1976 *(Not available at presstime.)*
Issue price: $50.00

Mother's Day Series

Diameter: 7½ inches. Limited by edition size of 7,500. Numbered without certificate.

22-69-5.1
1976 *Mother and Children.*
Artist: Leslie DeMille. Issue price: $40.00

The Nobility of Children Series

Artist: Edna Hibel. Diameter: 10 inches. Limited by edition size of 12,750. Numbered with certificate.

22-69-6.1
1976 *La Contessa Isabella.*
Issue price: $120.00

GERMANY
ROYAL BAYREUTH (Tettau)

22-73-1.1

Royal Bayreuth is the oldest active porcelain manufacturer in Bavaria, having produced fine porcelain since 1794. The firm is now a subsidiary of Royal Tettau. Royal Bayreuth issed its first limited-edition Christmas plate in 1972. This series depicts Bavarian winter scenes. In 1973, the firm began the Mother's Day series with artwork by contemporary artists. A seven piece set of *Sun-Bonnet Babies* plates in 1974 was copied from plates issued prior to World War I but was clearly marked as a new edition by its 1974 backstamp. These are from paintings by Bertha L. Corbett who later illustrated the book *The Sun-Bonnet Babies Primer* by E. O. Grover.

All plates listed are made in porcelain. Back Hanger attached. Numbered without certificate.

Christmas Series
Diameter: 8 inches.

22-73-1.1
1972 *Carriage in the Village*.
Artist: Unknown — from old painting.
Limited by edition size of 4,000.
Issue price: $15.00

22-73-1.2
1973 *Snow Scene*.
Artist: Unknown — from old painting.
Limited by edition size of 5,000.
Issue price: $16.50

22-73-1.3
1974 *The Old Mill*.
Artist: Unknown — from old painting.
Limited by edition size of 4,000.
Issue price: $24.00

22-73-1.4
1975 *Forest Chalet 'Serenity'*.
Artist: Georg Rotger. Limited by edition size of 4,000. Issue price: $27.50

Mother's Day Series
Diameter: 7¾ inches

22-73-2.1
1973 *Consolation*.
Artist: Ozz Franka. Artist's signature appears on back of plate. Limited edition size of 4,000. Issue price: $16.50

22-73-2.2

GERMANY
ROYAL BAYREUTH

22-73-2.2
1974 *Young Americans.*
Artist: Leo Jansen. Artist's name appears on back of plate. Limited by edition size of 4,000. Issue price: $25.00

22-73-2.3
1975 *Young Americans II.*
Artist: Leo Jansen. Artist's signature appears on front of plate. Limited by edition size of 5,000. Issue price: $25.00

22-73-2.4
1976 *Young Americans III.*
Artist: Leo Jansen. Artist's signature appears on front of plate. Limited by edition size of 5,000. Issue price: $30.00

Sunbonnet Babies Set

Artist: Bertha L. Corbett.
Diameter: 7 inches. Limited by edition size of 15,000 sets.
Backstamped 1974.
Issue price: $120.00

22-73-3.1
1974 *Sunday.*

22-73-3.1
1974 *Monday.*

22-73-3.1
1974 *Tuesday.*

22-73-3.1
1974 *Wednesday.*

22-73-3.1
1974 *Thursday.*

22-73-3.1
1974 *Friday.*

22-73-3.1
1974 *Saturday.*

GERMANY
ROYALE (Hoxter)

22-77-1.1

Plates currently issued by Royale are produced by the Furstenberg factory (see Germany, FURSTENBERG). The 1969 to 1970 plates were produced by the Kaiser factory (see Germany, KAISER). Royale issues plaques and ornaments as well as plates and lead crystal items (see Germany, ROYALE GERMANIA). Royale's Christmas series of plates began in 1969. Both the Mother's Day series, depicting animal families, and the Father's Day series started in 1970. The artist for all series is Jack Polusynski.

All plates listed are made in porcelain decorated in cobalt blue underglaze. Since 1971, the Christmas series has been made in bas-relief; the Mother's Day and Father's Day series changed to this same technique in 1972. Diameter: 7½ inches. Foot rims pierced for hanging. Not numbered.

Christmas Plates

22-77-1.1
1969 *Christmas Fair in Ebeltoft.*
Limited by announced edition size of 6,000.
Issue price: $12.00

22-77-1.2
1970 *Midnight Mass at Kalundborg Church.*
Limited by announced edition size of 10,000.
Issue price: $13.00

22-77-1.3
1971 *Christmas Night in a Village.*
Limited by announced edition size of 8,000.
Issue price: $16.00

22-77-1.4
1972 *Elks.*
Limited by announced edition size of 8,000.
Issue price: $16.00

22-77-1.5
1973 *Christmas Dawn.*
Limited by announced edition size of 6,000.
Issue price: $20.00

22-77-1.6
1974 *Village at Christmas.*
Limited by announced edition size of 5,000.
Issue price: $22.00

22-77-1.7
1975 *Feeding Time.*
Limited by announced edition size of 5,000.
Issue price: $26.00

22-77-1.8
1976 *Christmas at the Seaport.*
Limited by announced edition size of 5,000.
Issue price: $27.50

22-77-2.1

GERMANY
ROYALE

Father's Day Series

22-77-2.1
1970 *U.S. Frigate Constitution.*
Limited by announced edition size of 5,000.
Issue price: $13.00

22-77-2.2
1971 *Man Fishing.*
Limited by announced edition size of 5,000.
Issue price: $13.00

22-77-2.3
1972 *Mountain Climber.*
Limited by announced edition size of 6,000.
Issue price: $16.00

22-77-2.4
1973 *Camping.*
Limited by announced edition size of 4,000.
Issue price: $18.00

22-77-2.5
1974 *Eagle.*
Limited by announced edition size of 2,500.
Issue price: $22.00

22-77-2.6
1975 *Regatta.*
Limited by announced edition size of 2,500.
Issue price: $26.00

22-77-2.7
1976 *Hunting Scene.*
Limited by announced edition size of 2,500.
Issue price: $27.50

GERMANY
ROYALE

22-77-3.1

Mother's Day Series

22-77-3.1
1970 *Swan and Brood.*
Limited by announced edition size of 6,000.
Issue price: $12.00

22-77-3.2
1971 *Doe and Fawn.*
Limited by announced edition size of 9,000.
Issue price: $13.00

22-77-3.3
1972 *Rabbit Family.*
Limited by announced edition size of 9,000.
Issue price: $16.00

22-77-3.4
1973 *Owl Family.*
Limited by announced edition size of 6,000.
Issue price: $18.00

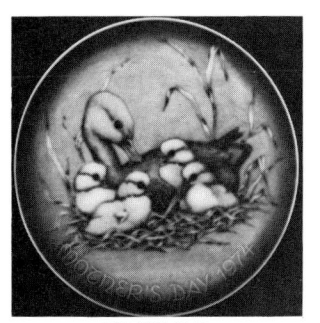

22-77-3.5
1974 *Duck Family.*
Limited by announced edition size of 5,000.
Issue price: $22.00

22-77-3.6
1975 *Lynx Family.*
Limited by announced edition size of 5,000.
Issue price: $26.00

22-77-3.7
1976 *Woodcock and Young.*
Limited by announced edition size of 5,000.
Issue price: $27.50

22-81-1.1
ROYALE GERMANIA (Schwabisch-Gmund)

GERMANY

Royale Germania plates are produced in the Josephine Hutte factory in southeast Germany. This factory, which dates back to the 14th century, is one of the oldest glass manufactories in Europe. Royale Germania is a division of Royale (see Germany, ROYALE). The firm makes goblets and paperweights in addition to limited-edition plates. The *Crystal Annual* series began in 1970 and ends in 1976. The *Crystal Mother's Day* series began in 1971 and similarly is completed in 1976. The artist for both series is Hans Negro.

All plates listed are handmade in full lead overlay crystal (white crystal with colored crystal). The plates are mouthblown, hand-cut, and copper-wheel engraved. Numbered without certificate.

Royale

Crystal Annual Series
Diameter: 8½ inches.

22-81-1.1
1970 *Orchid.*
Dark cobalt blue overlay. Edition size of 600. Issue price: $200.00

22-81-1.2
1971 *Cyclamen.*
Soft red overlay. Edition size of 1,000. Issue price: $200.00

22-81-1.3
1972 *Silver Thistle.*
Dark green overlay. Edition size of 1,000. Issue price: $250.00

22-81-1.4
1973 *Tulips.*
Pale lilac overlay. Edition size of 600. Issue price: $275.00

22-81-1.5
1974 *Sunflowers.*
Smokey topaz overlay. Edition size of 500. Issue price: $300.00

22-81-1.6
1975 *Flaming Heart.*
Amber overlay. Edition size of 350. Issue price: $450.00

GERMANY
ROYALE GERMANIA

22-81-2.1

*Crystal
Mother's Day Series*

Diameter: 6¼ inches.

22-81-2.1
1971 *Roses.*
Red overlay. Edition size of 250.
Issue price: $135.00

22-81-2.2
1972 *Elephant Mother and Baby.*
Dark green overlay. Edition size of 750.
Issue price: $180.00

22-81-2.3
1973 *Koala Bear and Cub.*
Pale lilac overlay. Edition size of 600.
Issue price: $200.00

22-81-2.4
1974 *Squirrels.*
Smokey topaz overlay. Edition size of 500.
Issue price: $240.00

22-81-2.5
1975 *Swan Family.*
Amber overlay. Edition size of 350.
Issue price: $350.00

22-85-1.1
SCHMID BROS. (Selb)

GERMANY

Schmid Bros. was established in Boston in the 1930s. Since then the firm has been a specialized importer of quality porcelain bells and mugs as well as plates. Schmid Bros. limited-edition plates are produced by the Hutschenreuther factory in Germany, noted for its porcelain figurines and tableware. The artwork for both the Christmas series and the Mother's Day series is by the late Berta Hummel created before she entered the Franciscan convent at Siessen in 1934 (see Germany, GOEBEL). The Christmas series was introduced in 1971 and the Mother's Day series in 1972.

All plates listed are made in porcelain. Diameter: 7¾ inches. Foot rims pierced for hanging. Limited by year of issue. Edition size undisclosed. Not numbered. Artist's signature or initials appear on front of plate up to 1974.

Schmid

Christmas Series

22-85-1.1
1971 *Angel in a Christmas Setting.*
Issue price: $15.00

22-85-1.2
1972 *Angel with Flute.*
Issue price: $15.00

22-85-1.3
1973 *The Nativity.*
Issue price: $15.00

22-85-1.4
1974 *The Guardian Angel.*
Issue price: $18.50

22-85-1.5
1975 *Christmas Child.*
Issue price: $25.00

22-85-1.6
1976 *Sacred Journey.*
Issue price: $27.50

GERMANY
SCHMID BROS.

22-85-2.1

Mother's Day Series

22-85-2.1
1972 *Playing Hooky.*
Issue price: $15.00

22-85-2.2
1973 *The Little Fisherman.*
Issue price: $15.00

22-85-2.3
1974 *The Bumblebee.*
Issue price: $18.50

22-85-2.4
1975 *Message of Love.*
Issue price: $25.00

22-85-2.5
1976 *Devotion for Mother.*
Issue price: $27.50

26-69-1.1
ROYAL DOULTON (Burslem, Stoke-on-Trent, Staffordshire)

GREAT BRITAIN

Doulton & Co. traces its beginnings in 1815 to the small stoneware pottery of John Doulton and John Watts near Vauxhall Gardens, London. In 1826, the pottery was moved to Lambeth and then finally to Burslem in 1877. There Doulton took over an established factory and began producing fine earthenware and china items. The company received the King's warrant in 1901, giving it authority to use "Royal" with its name.

The Royal Doulton Christmas plate series was the first issue in the *Collectors International* series. The Christmas series, begun in 1972, is fired at Royal Doulton's John Beswick Potteries and is of Christmas scenes in different countries around the world. These plates are made in earthenware in hand-cast bas-relief and are hand-painted in 15 colors.

The *Collectors International* series also includes the Mother's Day series begun in 1973. The paintings are by contemporary American artist Edna Hibel of mothers and children of various nations. Other series in the *Collectors International* series are also by contemporary artists. These plates are made in bone china. The artist's signature appears on front of plate, except Mother's Day series where it is on back.

Christmas Series

Size: 8" by 8" square. Foot rims pierced for hanging. Not numbered. Limited by announced edition size of 15,000.

26-69-1.1
1972 *Christmas in England.*
Artist: Harry Sales. Issue price: $35.00

26-69-1.2
1973 *Christmas in Mexico.*
Artist: Chavela Castrejon. Issue price: $37.50

26-69-1.3
1974 *Christmas in Bulgaria.*
Artist: Dimitri Yordanov. Issue price: $37.50

26-69-1.4
1975 *Christmas in Norway.*
Artist: Alton Toby. Issue price: $45.00

26-69-1.5
1976 *Christmas in Holland.*
Artist: Alton Toby. Issue price: $50.00

GREAT BRITAIN
ROYAL DOULTON

26-69-2.1

Mother's Day Series

Diameter: 8¼ inches. Not numbered. Limited by announced edition size of 15,000.

26-69-2.1
1973 *Colette and Child.*
Issue price: $40.00

26-69-2.2
1974 *Sayuri and Child.*
Issue price: $40.00

26-69-2.3
1975 *Kristina and Child.*
Issue price: $50.00

26-69-2.4
1976 *Marilyn and Child.*
Issue price: $55.00

Commedia Dell' Arte Series

Diameter: 10 inches. Artist: LeRoy Neiman. Numbered without certificate. Limited by edition size of 15,000. Planned series of four.

26-69-3.1
1974 *Harlequin.*
Issue price: $50.00

26-69-3.2
1976 *Pierrot.*
Issue price: $60.00

26-69-4.1

GREAT BRITAIN
ROYAL DOULTON

Flower Garden Series

Diameter: 10 inches. Artist: Hahn Vidal. Numbered without certificate. Limited by edition size of 15,000.

26-69-4.1
1975 *Spring Harmony.*
Issue price: $60.00

26-69-4.2
1976 *Dreaming Lotus.*
Issue price: $65.00

Ports of Call Series

Diameter: 10 inches. Artist: Doug Kingman. Numbered without certificate. Limited by edition size of 15,000.

26-69-5.1
1975 *Fisherman's Wharf (San Francisco).*
Issue price: $60.00

26-69-5.2
1976 *Royal Street (New Orleans).*
Issue price: $65.00

GREAT BRITAIN
ROYAL DOULTON

The Log of the "Dashing Wave" Series

Diameter: 10 inches. Artist: John Stobart. Numbered without certificate. Limited by edition size of 15,000.

26-69-6.1
1976 *Sailing with the Tide.*
Issue price: $65.00

Valentine's Day Series

Diameter: 8¼ inches. Limited by period of issue. Edition size undisclosed. Not numbered.

26-69-7.1
1976 *Victorian Boy and Girl.*
From an old print. Issue price: $25.00

26-78-1.1
ROYAL WORCESTER (Worcester)

GREAT BRITAIN

The Worcester Porcelain Company was established in 1751 by a group led by Dr. John Wall, physician and amateur artist, and William Davis, an apothecary, after they perfected a formula for making soft paste porcelain from steatite. George III gave the company permission to call itself "China Manufacturers to their Majesties" in 1788. After undergoing several changes in ownership the firm was reorganized in 1862 as the Royal Worcester Porcelain Company. During the early 1900s Royal Worcester began to manufacture bone china items.

In 1972, Royal Worcester introduced a series of 12 dessert plates based on the porcelain sculptures of American Birds by Dorothy Doughty. Collector's plates of bone china are produced in Worcester, England, those of pewter in the United States (see United States, ROYAL WORCESTER).

All plates listed are made in bone china in bas-relief and are hand-painted. Diameter 8 inches. Not numbered. Artist's name appears on back.

Doughty Bird Series

26-78-1.1
1972 *Redstarts and Beech.*
Limited by announced edition size of 2,750.
Issue price: $125.00

26-78-1.2
1973 *Myrtle Warbler and Cherry.*
Limited by announced edition size of 3,000.
Issue price: $175.00

26-78-1.3
1974 *Blue-Grey Gnatcatchers.*
Limited by announced edition size of 3,000.
Issue price: $195.00

26-78-1.4
1975 *Blackburnian Warbler.*
Limited by announced edition size of 3,000.
Issue price: $235.00

26-78-1.5
1976 *Blue-Winged Sivas and Bamboo.*
Limited by announced edition size of 3,000.
Issue price: $195.00

GREAT BRITAIN
SPODE (Stoke-on-Trent, Staffordshire)

26-86-1.1

Josiah Spode established his pottery, The Spode Works in 1770, at Stoke-on-Trent. In experimentation Spode added bone ash to the porcelain formula and the resultant ceramic became known as bone china. It has since become the standard English china. Upon Spode's death in 1797 his son, Josiah Spode II, continued his work, with William Copeland in charge of sales. Eventually Copeland became sole owner, and from 1847 descendents of William Copeland operated the firm, calling it W. T. Copeland & Sons, Ltd. In 1967, W. T. Copeland & Sons was purchased by The Carborundum Co. The Spode trademark has been retained and the present factory is located on the same site as the original pottery.

Spode's Christmas plate series, with artwork by Gillian West, began in 1970, drawing its theme from old English carols. The plate design is from an original 18th century Spode model. Decorations of the 1970 and 1971 plates are in gold; thereafter decorations are gold with a second color which is changed every two years.

All plates listed are made in bone china. Diameter: 8 inches. Limited by year of issue. Edition size undisclosed. Not numbered.

Christmas Series

26-86-1.1
1970 *Partridge in a Pear Tree.*
Issue price: $35.00

26-86-1.2
1971 *In Heaven the Angels Singing.*
Issue price: $35.00

26-86-1.3
1972 *We Saw Three Ships A-Sailing.*
Issue price: $35.00

26-86-1.4
1973 *We Three Kings of Orient Are.*
Issue price: $35.00

26-86-1.5
1974 *Deck the Halls.*
Issue price: $35.00

26-86-1.6
1975 *Christbaum.*
Issue price: $45.00

26-86-1.7
1976 *Good King Wenceslas.*
Issue price: $45.00

26-90-1.1
WEDGWOOD (Balaston, Stoke-on-Trent, Staffordshire)

GREAT BRITAIN

Josiah Wedgwood established his firm in Burslem in 1759. He is often called "the father of English potters" because of his innovations, particularly that of Jasperware, the most widely collected of his works. Jasperware is unglazed stoneware with stained blue, green, lilac, yellow, maroon, or black backgrounds and hand-applied white Jasper ornamentation for a cameo effect. Josiah Wedgwood & Sons, Ltd., located in Barlaston since 1940, began in 1969 the first English collector's Christmas plate series in traditional "Wedgwood blue". This series of famous English monuments commemorates the bicentennial of the second Wedgwood factory. The modeler is Tom Harper. The Mother's Day series, started in 1971, reproduces designs created for Wedgwood by 18th-century artists. The Wedgwood *American Bicentennial* series, depicting events that led to American Independence, began in 1972. This six-plate series is in blue Jasperware. The modeler for this series is undisclosed.

All plates listed are Jasperware. Limited by year of issue. Edition size undisclosed. Not numbered.

Christmas Series
Diameter: 8 inches.

26-90-1.1
1969 *Windsor Castle.*
Issue price: $25.00

26-90-1.2
1970 *Christmas in Trafalgar Square.*
Issue price: $30.00

26-90-1.3
1971 *Picadilly Circus, London.*
Issue price: $30.00

26-90-1.4
1972 *St. Paul's Cathedral.*
Issue price: $35.00

26-90-1.5
1973 *The Tower of London.*
Issue price: $40.00

26-90-1.6
1974 *The Houses of Parliament.*
Issue price: $40.00

26-90-1.7
1975 *Tower Bridge.*
Issue price: $45.00

GREAT BRITAIN
WEDGWOOD

26-90-2.1

Mother's Day Series

Diameter: 6½ inches.

26-90-2.1
1971 *Sportive Love.*
Reproduces design by Lady Elizabeth Templetown. Black Jasper.
Issue price: $20.00

26-90-2.2
1972 *The Sewing Lesson.*
Reproduces design by Emma Crewe. Sage green Jasper. Issue price: $20.00

26-90-2.3
1973 *The Baptism of Achilles.*
Reproduces design by Lady Elizabeth Templetown. Pale blue Jasper.
Issue price: $25.00

26-90-2.4
1974 *Domestic Employment.*
Reproduces design by Lady Elizabeth Templetown. Pale blue Jasper.
Issue price: $30.00

26-90-2.5
1975 *Mother and Child.*
Reproduces design by Lady Elizabeth Templetown. Portland blue Jasper.
Issue price: $35.00

26-90-2.6
1976 *The Spinner.*
Reproduces design by William Hackwood. Pale blue Jasper. Issue price: $35.00

26-90-3.1

GREAT BRITAIN
WEDGWOOD

Bicentennial Series

Diameter: 8 inches.

26-90-3.1
1972 *Boston Tea Party.*
Issue price: $30.00

26-90-3.2
1973 *Paul Revere's Ride.*
Issue price: $35.00

26-90-3.3
1974 *Battle of Concord.*
Issue price: $40.00

26-90-3.4
1975 *Across the Delaware.*
Issue price: $45.00

26-90-3.5
1975 *Victory at Yorktown.*
Issue price: $40.00

26-90-3.6
1976 *Declaration Signed.*
Issue price: $45.00

IRELAND
BELLEEK (Belleek, County Fermanagh)

34-8-1.1

Belleek Pottery Ltd. was established in 1857 by David McBirney and Robert W. Armstrong on an island in the River Erne. This site is near deposits of feldspathic clay which produces an iridescent effect when metallic washes are applied. The firm has used this technique in tea sets, figurines, baskets, and other items. The designs have often been based on the shamrock or marine life. During the 1880s and 1890s some workers from Belleek were brought to the United States to produce an American Belleek which was heavier and less translucent. In 1970, Belleek of Ireland introduced its Christmas plate series based on Irish subjects. Names of artists undisclosed.

All plates listed are made in parian china that is thin cream-colored with an iridescent luster. Each plate is embossed with molded designs. Diameter: 7½ inches. Limited by announced edition size of 5,000.

Christmas Series

34-8-1.1
1970 *Castle Caldwell.*
Issue price: $25.00

34-8-1.2
1971 *Celtic Cross.*
Issue price: $25.00

34-8-1.3
1972 *Flight of the Earls.*
Issue price: $30.00

34-8-1.4
1973 *Tribute to W. B. Yeats.*
Issue price: $38.50

34-8-1.5
1974 *Devenish Island.*
Issue price: $45.00

34-8-1.6
1975 *The Celtic Cross.*
Issue price: $48.00

38-4-1.1
ANRI (Santa Christina)

ITALY

The House of Anri, which claims to be the world's largest woodcarving manufactory, was established in 1916 by Anton Fiffeser, Sr. The factory is located in the Tyrolean Alps, an area with a long heritage of woodcarving families. The firm is now run by Anton Fiffeser, Jr. Anri's Christmas series was introduced in 1971. The Mother's Day and the Father's Day series both began in 1972. Names of artists undisclosed.

All plates listed are hand-carved in wood and hand-painted to produce a three-dimensional effect. Each plate is mounted in a circular European maple frame. Back hanger attached. Numbered without certificate.

Christmas Series

Diameter: 12 inches. Limited by edition size of 10,000 from 1972.

38-4-1.1
1971 *St. Jakob in Groden.*
Limited by announced edition size of 10,000.
Issue price: $37.50

38-4-1.2
1972 *Pipers at Alberobello.*
Issue price: $45.00

38-4-1.3
1973 *Alpine Horn.*
Issue price: $45.00

38-4-1.4
1974 *Young Man and Girl.*
Issue price: $50.00

38-4-1.5
1975 *Christmas in Ireland.*
Issue price: $60.00

38-4-1.6
1976 *Alpine Christmas.*
Issue price: $65.00

ITALY
ANRI

38-4-2.1

Father's Day Series

Diameter: 9 inches. Limited by edition size of 5,000.

38-4-2.1
1972 *Alpine Father and Children.*
Issue price: $35.00

38-4-2.2
1973 *Alpine Father and Children.*
Issue price: $40.00

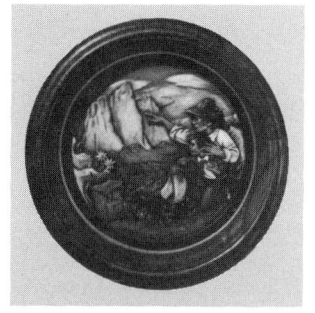

38-4-2.3
1974 *Cliff Gazing.*
Issue price: $50.00

38-4-2.4
1975 *Sailing.*
Issue price: $60.00

38-4-3.1

ITALY
ANRI

Mother's Day Series

Diameter: 9 inches. Limited by edition size of 5,000.

38-4-3.1
1972 *Alpine Mother and Children.*
Issue price: $35.00

38-4-3.2
1973 *Alpine Mother and Children.*
Issue price: $40.00

38-4-3.3
1974 *Alpine Mother and Children.*
Issue price: $50.00

38-4-3.4
1975 *Alpine Stroll.*
Issue price: $60.00

38-4-3.5
1976 *Knitting.*
Issue price: $60.00

ITALY
KING'S (Usmate, Milan)

38-43-1.1

King's Porcelain was established in the original Giuseppe Cappe factory in the 1960s. The factory had been known for its Cappe figurines of which King's has retained the original figurine molds. In 1973, King's initiated three series of collector's plates: The Christmas series, Mother's Day series and *Flowers of America* series.

All plates listed are made in porcelain in high relief and hand-painted with a gold border. Diameter: 8¾ inches. Foot rims pierced for hanging. Numbered without certificate.

Christmas Series
Limited by edition size of 1,500.

38-43-1.1
1973 *Adoration of Christ.*
Artist: Bruno Merli. Issue price: $150.00

38-43-1.2
1974 *Madonna.*
Artist: Bruno Merli. Issue price: $150.00

38-43-1.3
1975 *Heavenly Choir.*
Artist: Aldo Falchi. Issue price: $160.00

38-43-1.4
1976 *Little Girl and her Brother.*
Artist: Aldo Falchi. Limited by edition size of 100. Issue price: $200.00

Flowers of America Series
Limited by edition size of 1,000.
Artist: Sandro Varnazza.

38-43-2.1
1973 *Pink Carnation.*
Issue price: $85.00

38-43-2.2
1974 *Red Roses.*
Issue price: $100.00

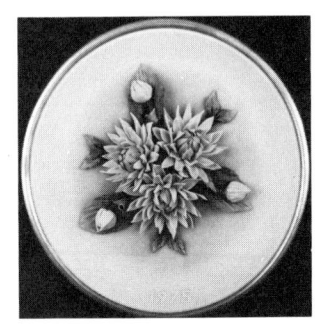

38-43-2.3

ITALY
KINGS

38-43-2.3
1975 *Yellow Dahlia.*
Issue price: $110.00

38-43-2.4
1976 *Bluebells.*
Artist: Sandro Vernazza. Limited by edition size of 750. Issue price: $130.00

Mother's Day Series

Limited by edition size of 1,500.

38-43-3.1
1973 *Dancing Girl.*
Artist: Bruno Merli. Issue price: $100.00

38-43-3.2
1974 *Dancing Boy.*
Artist: Bruno Merli. Issue price: $115.00

38-43-3.3
1975 *Motherly Love.*
Artist: Aldo Falchi. Issue price: $140.00

38-43-3.4
1976 *Maiden.*
Artist: Aldo Falchi. Limited by edition size of 1,000. Issue price: $180.00

ITALY
STUDIO DANTE di VOLTERADICI (Volterra)

38-72-1.1

The Studio Dante de Volteradici continues the Italian tradition of alabaster sculpturing. It is located near Tuscany, long the world center for the mining and carving of alabaster. The Studio's *Grand Opera* series commemorating the 200th anniversary of La Scala Opera House began in 1976. The artist is Gino Ruggeri.

Plate listed is made in Ivory Alabaster in high relief. Diameter: 8½ inches. Back hanger attached. Limited by announced period of issue. Edition size undisclosed. Numbered with certificate. Artist's name appears on front and back of plate.

St.º Dante di Volteradici

Grand Opera Series

38-72-1.1
1976 *Rigoletto.*
Issue price: $35.00

38-84-1.1
VENETO FLAIR/CREATIVE WORLD (Treviso)

ITALY

The Veneto Flair factory was established in 1946 by a consortium of painters and pottery-artisans. Creative World, New York City, is the American importer and distributor of Veneto Flair plates. Veneto Flair plates are made by a centuries-old technique: Each plate is modeled by hand on a potter's wheel and hand-engraved. A mosaic effect is then achieved by a protracted series of paintings and firings. The artist for all series is Vincente Tiziano.

All plates listed are made in terra cotta. Foot rims pierced for hanging. Numbered with certificate.

Bellini Plate
Diameter: 8½ inches.

38-84-1.1
1971 *Madonna.*
Limited by edition size of 500.
Issue price: $37.50

Christmas Series
Diameter: 8½ inches.

38-84-2.1
1971 *Three Kings.*
Limited by edition size of 1,500.
Issue price: $45.00

38-84-2.2
1972 *Shepherds.*
Limited by edition size of 2,000.
Issue price: $45.00

38-84-2.3
1973 *Christ Child.*
Limited by edition size of 2,000.
Issue price: $55.00

38-84-2.4
1974 *Angel.*
Limited by edition size of 2,000.
Issue price: $55.00

Wildlife Series
Diameter: 8½ inches.
Four-plate series.

38-84-3.1
1971 *Deer.*
Limited by edition size of 500.
Issue price: $37.50

ITALY
VENETO FLAIR

38-84-3.2

38-84-3.2
1972 *Elephant.*
Limited by edition size of 1,000.
Issue price: $37.50

38-84-3.3
1973 *Puma.*
Limited by edition size of 2,000.
Issue price: $37.50

38-84-3.4
1974 *Tiger.*
Limited by edition size of 2,000.
Issue price: $40.00

Bird Series

Diameter: 8½ inches. Limited by edition size of 2,000. Three-plate series.

38-84-4.1
1972 *Owl.*
Issue price: $37.50

38-84-4.2
1973 *Falcon.*
Issue price: $37.50

38-84-4.3
1974 *Mallard.*
Issue price: $45.00

Dog Series

Diameter: 8½ inches. Limited by edition size of 2,000. Four-plate series.

38-84-5.1
1972 *German Shepherd.*
Issue price: $37.50

38-84-5.2
1973 *Poodle.*
Issue price: $37.50

38-84-5.3
1974 *Doberman.*
Issue price: $40.00

38-84-5.4
1975 *Collie.*
Issue price: $45.00

38-84-5.6

ITALY
VENETO FLAIR

38-84-5.5
1976 *Dashshund.*
Issue price: $45.00

Last Supper Series

Diameter: 8½ inches. Limited by edition size of 2,000. Five-plate series. Based on Leonardo da Vinci's *Last Supper.*

38-84-6.1
1972 *Three Apostles.*
Issue price: $100.00

38-84-6.2
1973 *Three Apostles.*
Issue price: $70.00

38-84-6.3
1974 *Three Apostles.*
Issue price: $70.00

38-84-6.4
1975 *Three Apostles.*
Issue price: $70.00

38-84-6.5
1976 *Christ.*
Issue price: $70.00

Mother's Day Series

Diameter: 8½ inches. Limited by edition size of 2,000.

38-84-7.1
1972 *Madonna & Child.*
Issue price: $55.00

38-84-7.2
1973 *Madonna & Child.*
Issue price: $55.00

ITALY
VENETO FLAIR

38-84-7.3

38-84-7.3
1974 *Mother and Son.*
Issue price: $55.00

38-84-7.4
1975 *Daughter and Doll.*
Issue price: $45.00

Maker had
no photo at
presstime

38-84-7.5
1976 *Son and Daughter.*
Issue price: $55.00

Easter Series

Diameter: 8½ inches. Limited by edition size of 2,000.

38-84-8.1
1973 *Rabbits.*
Issue price: $50.00

38-84-8.2
1974 *Chicks.*
Issue price: $50.00

38-84-8.3
1975 *Lamb.*
Issue price: $50.00

38-84-8.4
1976 *Composite.*
Issue price: $70.00

38-84-9.1

ITALY
VENETO FLAIR

Mosaic Series
Diameter: 6½ inches.

38-84-9.1
1973 *Justinian.*
Limited by edition size of 500.
Issue price: $50.00

38-84-9.2
1974 *Pelican.*
Limited by edition size of 1,000.
Issue price: $50.00

Cat Series
Diameter: 8½ inches. Limited by edition size of 2,000.

38-84-10.1
1974 *Persian.*
Issue price: $40.00

38-84-10.2
1975 *Siamese.*
Issue price: $45.00

38-84-10.3
1976 *Tabby.*
Issue price: $45.00

Christmas Card Series
Diameter: 7¼ inches.
Four-plate series.

38-84-11.1
1975 *Christmas Eve.*
Limited by edition size of 5,000.
Issue price: $45.00

38-84-11.2
1976 *The Old North Church.*
Issue price: $45.00

JAPAN
SANGO (Nagoya)

42-72-1.1

The Sango Porcelain factory was established by the Katoh family after World War II. The factory produces various hard-fire porcelain ware. The *Living American Artists* series began in 1976. Plate listed is made in porcelain with 7/8 inch gold filigree border. Diameter: 10½ inches. Limited by edition size of 10,000. Numbered without certificate. Artist's name appears on front of plate.

Sango

Living American Artists Series

42-72-1.1
1976 *Sweethearts.*
Artist: Norman Rockwell. Issue price: $30.00

Mother's Day Series

Diameter: 7-5/8 inches. Limited by edition size of 7,500. Numbered without certificate.

42-72-2.1
1976 *Spring Delight.*
Artist: Gloria Ranck. Issue price: $20.00

42-85-1.1
SCHMID BROS. (Tajimi City, Gifu)

JAPAN

A Japanese subsidiary of Schmid Bros. (see Germany, SCHMID BROS.) produces several series of plates based on contemporary cartoon characters. The *Disney* Christmas series began in 1973 and the *Disney* Mother's Day series in 1974. Artwork for these series is by the Walt Disney Syndicate. The *Peanuts* Christmas series and the *Peanuts* Mother's Day series began in 1972 using artwork designed or approved by Charles Schultz. The Schultz name appears on the front of each plate.

All plates listed are made in porcelain. Diameter: 7½ inches. Back hanger attached on recent issues. Limited by year of issue. Edition size undisclosed. Not numbered.

Peanuts Christmas Series

42-85-1.1
1972 *Snoopy Guides the Sleigh.*
Issue price: $10.00

42-85-1.2
1973 *Christmas Eve at the Doghouse.*
Issue price: $10.00

42-85-1.3
1974 *Christmas Eve at the Fireplace.*
Issue price: $10.00

42-85-1.4
1975 *Woodstock, Santa Claus.*
Issue price: $12.50

42-85-1.5
1976 *Woodstock's Christmas.*
Issue price: $13.00

JAPAN
SCHMID BROS.

42-85-2.1

Peanuts Mother's Day Series

42-85-2.1
1972 *Charlie Brown.*
Issue price: $10.00

42-85-2.2
1973 *Mom ?*
Issue price: $10.00

42-85-2.3
1974 *Snoopy & Woodstock on Parade.*
Issue price: $10.00

42-85-2.4
1975 *A Kiss for Lucy.*
Issue price: $12.50

42-85-2.5
1976 *Linus and Snoopy.*
Issue price: $13.00

Disney Christmas Series

42-85-3.1
1973 *Sleigh-ride.*
Issue price: $10.00

42-85-3.2
1974 *Decorating the Tree.*
Issue price: $10.00

42-85-3.3

JAPAN
SCHMID BROS.

42-85-3.3
1975 *Caroling.*
Issue price: $12.50

42-85-3.4
1976 *Building a Snowman.*
Issue price: $13.00

*Disney
Mother's Day Series*

42-85-4.1
1974 *Flowers for Mother.*
Issue price: $10.00

42-85-4.2
1975 *Snow White & the Seven Dwarfs.*
Issue price: $12.50

42-85-4.3
1976 *Minnie Mouse and Friends.*
Issue price: $13.00

NORWAY
PORSGRUND (Porsgrunn, Tellemark County)

54-61-1.1

Porsgrund, Norway's only porcelain factory, was established in 1885 by Jeremiason Johan. Johan, a shipowner, began his business by importing English clay which was modeled by ceramist Carl Bauer. Porcelain tableware and decorative wares have been produced since then. In 1909, Porsgrund produced a small edition of a Christmas plate entitled *Christmas Flowers*. In 1968, a new Christmas series was introduced. The Mother's Day series began in 1971 and the Easter series in 1972. Artist for all series is Gunnar Bratlie.

All plates listed are made in porcelain decorated in cobalt blue underglaze. Foot rims pierced for hanging. Limited by year of issue. Edition size undisclosed. Not numbered.

Christmas Series
Diameter: 7 inches.

54-61-1.1
1968 *Church Scene.*
Issue price: $12.00

54-61-1.2
1969 *Three Kings.*
Issue price: $12.00

54-61-1.3
1970 *Road to Bethlehem.*
Issue price: $12.00

54-61-1.4
1971 *A Child is Born in Bethlehem.*
Issue price: $12.00

54-61-1.5
1972 *Hark, the Herald Angels Sing.*
Issue price: $12.00

54-61-1.6
1973 *Promise of the Savior.*
Issue price: $15.00

54-61-1.7
1974 *The Shepherds.*
Issue price: $15.00

54-61-1.8
1975 *Jesus on the Road to the Temple.*
Issue price: $19.50

54-61-1.9

NORWAY
PORSGRUND

54-61-1.9
1976 *Jesus and the Elders.*
Issue price: $22.00

Mother's Day Series

Diameter: 5 inches.

54-61-2.1
1970 *Mare and Foal.*
Issue price: $7.50

54-61-2.2
1971 *Boy and Geese.*
Issue price: $7.50

54-61-2.3
1972 *Doe and Fawn.*
Issue price: $10.00

54-61-2.4
1973 *Cat and Kittens.*
Issue price: $10.00

54-61-2.5
1974 *Boy and Goats.*
Issue price: $10.00

54-61-2.6
1975 *Dog and Puppies.*
Issue price: $12.50

54-61-2.7
1976 *Girl and Calf.*
Issue price: $15.00

NORWAY
PORSGRUND

54-61-3.1

Father's Day Series

Diameter: 5 inches.

54-61-3.1
1971 *Fishing.*
Issue price: $10.00

54-61-3.2
1972 *Cookout.*
Issue price: $10.00

54-61-3.3
1973 *Sledding.*
Issue price: $10.00

54-61-3.4
1974 *Father and Son.*
Issue price: $10.00

54-61-3.5
1975 *Skating.*
Issue price: $12.50

54-61-3.6
1976 *Skiing.*
Issue price: $15.00

54-61-4.1

NORWAY
PORSGRUND

Easter Series

Diameter: 7 inches.

54-61-4.1
1972 *Ducks.*
Issue price: $12.00

54-61-4.2
1973 *Birds.*
Issue price: $12.00

54-61-4.3
1974 *Bunnies.*
Issue price: $15.00

54-61-4.4
1975 *Chicks.*
Issue price: $19.50

54-61-4.5
1976 *Sheep in the Field.*
Issue price: $22.00

SPAIN
LLADRO (Tabernes Blanques, Valencia)

72-46-1.1

The Lladro Porcelain factory was established in the 1950s by the three Lladro brothers — Juan, Jose, and Vincente. Sons of a peasant, they studied porcelain designing, modeling, and firing at night. The brothers built their first kiln while in their teens. By 1970, their factory was one of the best-equipped in Europe and had become known for its vases and figurines. Lladro initiated both its limited-edition Christmas series and Mother's Day series in 1971. Artist for both series is Juan Lladro.

All plates listed are hand-made in bas-relief white bisque in the center, with gray or blue underglaze porcelain borders and 14k gold trim. Diameter: 8 inches. Limited by year of issue. Edition size undisclosed. Not numbered.

LLADRÓ

Christmas Series

72-46-1.1
1971 *Caroling.*
Issue price: $27.50

72-46-1.2
1972 *Carolers.*
Issue price: $35.00

72-46-1.3
1973 *Boy and Girl.*
Issue price: $45.00

72-46-1.4
1974 *Carolers.*
Issue price: $55.00

72-46-1.5
1975 *Cherubs.*
Issue price: $60.00

72-46-2.1

SPAIN
LLADRO

Mother's Day Series

72-46-2.1
1971 *Kiss of the Child.*
Issue price: $27.50

72-46-2.2
1972 *Bird and Chicks.*
Issue price: $27.50

72-46-2.3
1973 *Mother and Children.*
Issue price: $35.00

72-46-2.4
1974 *Mother Nursing.*
Issue price: $45.00

72-46-2.5
1975 *Mother and Child.*
Issue price: $60.00

Maker had
no photo at
presstime

72-46-2.6
1976 *Mother and Baby.*
Issue price: $60.00

SPAIN
SANTA CLARA (undisclosed)

72-72-1.1

Santa Clara porcelain comes from an undisclosed factory in Spain, claimed to be one of the world's oldest. The Santa Clara Christmas series began in 1970. Name of artist undisclosed.

All plates listed are made in porcelain in cobalt blue and white underglaze with 24k gold decoration. Diameter: 8 inches. Foot rims pierced for hanging. Numbered without certificate since 1971.

Christmas Series

72-72-1.1
1970 *Christmas Message.*
Limited by announced edition size of 10,000.
Issue price: $18.00

72-72-1.2
1971 *Three Wise Men.*
Limited by edition size of 10,000.
Issue price: $18.00

72-72-1.3
1972 *Children in the Woods.*
Limited by edition size of 10,000.
Issue price: $20.00

72-72-1.4
1973 *Archangel.*
Limited by edition size of 5,000.
Issue price: $25.00

72-72-1.5
1974 *Spirit of Christmas.*
Limited by edition size of 5,000.
Issue price: $25.00

72-72-1.6
1975 *Christmas Eve in the Country.*
Limited by edition size of 5,000.
Issue price: $27.50

76-57-1.1
ORREFORS (Orrefors, Smaland)

SWEDEN

Orrefors Glassworks was established in 1916 in the forests of Smaland province. The first pieces of the Glassworks exhibited at international shows were acclaimed as elegant and distinctive. Orrefors crystal comes from a mixture of seashore sand and potash, plus a heavy lead content. The ornamentation is created by master blowers who apply liquid molten glass in desired shapes which are then finished on an engraver's wheel. In 1970, the firm began its *Annual Cathedral* series in clear crystal. The series depicts famous places of worship. In 1971, Orrefors introduced the Mother's Day series executed in deep blue crystal. Artist for all series is John Selbing.

All plates listed are entirely hand-made in leaded crystal with engraved designs inlaid with 24k gold. This manufacturing technique was developed by John Selbing. Numbered since 1975 without certificate.

Annual Cathedral Series

Diameter: 10 inches. Limited by announced edition size of 5,000 through 1974.

76-57-1.1
1970 *Notre Dame Cathedral.*
Issue price: $50.00

76-57-1.2
1971 *Westminster Abbey.*
Issue price: $50.00

76-57-1.3
1972 *Basilica di San Marco.*
Issue price: $50.00

76-57-1.4
1973 *Cologne Cathedral.*
Issue price: $50.00

76-57-1.5
1974 *Temple Rue de la Victoire, Paris.*
Issue price: $60.00

76-57-1.6
1975 *Basilica di San Pietro, Rome.*
Limited by edition size of 5,000.
Issue price: $85.00

76-57-1.7
1976 *Christ Church, Philadelphia.*
Issue price: $85.00

SWEDEN
ORREFORS

76-57-2.1

Mother's Day Series

Diameter: 8 inches. Limited by announced edition size of 2,500 through 1974.

76-57-2.1
1971 *Flowers for Mother.*
Issue price: $45.00

76-57-2.2
1972 *Mother and Children.*
Issue price: $45.00

76-57-2.3
1973 *Mother and Child.*
Issue price: $50.00

76-57-2.4
1974 *Mother and Child.*
Issue price: $50.00

76-57-2.5
1975 *Mother and Child.*
Limited by edition size of 3,000.
Issue price: $60.00

Maker had no photo at presstime

76-57-2.6
1976 *Children and Puppy.*
Issue price: $50.00

76-69-1.1
RORSTRAND (Lidkoping)

SWEDEN

The Rorstrand Porcelain Factory was established with government patronage near Stockholm in 1726. It is Sweden's oldest porcelain factory and the second oldest in Europe. The firm's products include dinnerware, kitchenware, wall plaques, and other decorative art, in addition to porcelain collector's plates. Rorstrand also produces ceramics made of stoneware and high-fired earthenware. The plant was moved to inland Lidkoping during World War II. Rorstrand, which had manufactured Christmas plates from 1904 to 1926, initiated its present Christmas series in 1968. The Mother's Day series was begun in 1971. The Father's Day series ran from 1971 to 1974. Designs for all series are derived from Swedish folk traditions and tales.

All plates listed are made in porcelain decorated in Scandia blue underglaze. Foot rims pierced for hanging. Limited by year of issue. Edition size undisclosed. Not numbered.

Christmas Series

7½ inch square plate.
Artist: Gunnar Nylund.

76-69-1.1
1968 *Bringing Home the Tree.*
Issue price: $12.00

76-69-1.2
1969 *Fisherman Sailing Home.*
Issue price: $13.50

76-69-1.3
1970 *Nils with His Geese.*
Issue price: $13.50

76-69-1.4
1971 *Nils in Lapland.*
Issue price: $15.00

76-69-1.5
1972 *Dalecarlian Fiddler.*
Issue price: $15.00

76-69-1.6
1973 *Farm in Smaland.*
Issue price: $16.00

76-69-1.7
1974 *Vadstena.*
Issue price: $19.00

76-69-1.8
1975 *Nils in Vastmanland.*
Issue price: $20.00

SWEDEN
RORSTRAND

76-69-2.1

Father's Day Series

Diameter: 8 inches. Artist: Carl Larsson. Artist's initials appear on front of plate.

76-69-2.1
1971 *Father and Child.*
Issue price: $15.00

76-69-2.2
1972 *Meal at Home.*
Issue price: $15.00

76-69-2.3
1973 *Tilling the Fields.*
Issue price: $16.00

76-69-2.4
1974 *Fishing.*
Issue price: $18.00

Mother's Day Series

Diameter: 8 inches. Artist: Carl Larsson. Artist's initials appear on front of plate.

76-69-3.1
1971 *Mother and Child.*
Issue price: $15.00

76-69-3.2
1972 *Shelling Peas.*
Issue price: $15.00

76-69-3.3
1973 *Old-fashioned Picnic.*
Issue price: $16.00

76-69-3.4

SWEDEN
RORSTRAND

76-69-3.4
1974 *Candle Lighting.*
Issue price: $18.00

76-69-3.5
1975 *Pontius on the Floor.*
Issue price: $20.00

UNITED STATES
FRANKLIN MINT (Franklin Center, Pennsylvania)

84-23-1.1

The Franklin Mint is considered to be the world's largest private mint with several international subsidiaries and branches. The firm was established in Philadelphia in 1965 by Joseph Segel. The Franklin Mint specializes in medallic art forms and produces coins for foreign governments. The six-plate *Rockwell* Christmas series in sterling silver with artwork by Norman Rockwell began in 1970 and was completed in 1975. In 1972, the Mother's Day series by artist Irene Spencer and the five-plate *James Wyeth Annual* series were introduced.

All plates listed are made in sterling silver and hand-etched. Diameter: 8 inches. Numbered with certificate. Artist's signature on front of plate.

Christmas Series
Artist: Norman Rockwell.

84-23-1.1
1970 *Bringing Home the Tree.*
Limited by edition size of 18,321.
Issue price: $100.00

84-23-1.2
1971 *Under the Mistletoe.*
Limited by edition size of 24,792.
Issue price: $100.00

84-23-1.3
1972 *The Carolers.*
Limited by edition size of 29,074.
Issue price: $125.00

84-23-1.4
1973 *Trimming the Tree.*
Limited by edition size of 18,010.
Issue price: $125.00

84-23-1.5
1974 *Hanging the Wreath.*
Limited by edition size of 12,822.
Issue price: $175.00

84-23-1.6
1975 *Home for Christmas.*
Issue price: $180.00

Mother's Day Series
Artist: Irene Spencer.

84-23-2.1
1972 *Mother and Child.*
Limited by edition size of 21,987.
Issue price: $125.00

84-23-2.2

UNITED STATES
FRANKLIN MINT

84-23-2.2
1973 *Mother and Child.*
Limited by edition size of 6,154.
Issue price: $125.00

84-23-2.3
1974 *Mother and Child.*
Limited by edition size of 5,116.
Issue price: $150.00

84-23-2.4
1975 *Mother and Child.*
Limited by edition size of 2,704.
Issue price: $187.50

Wyeth Annual Series

Artist: James Wyeth.

84-23-3.1
1972 *Along the Brandywine.*
Limited by edition size of 19,670.
Issue price: $125.00

84-23-3.2
1973 *Winter Fox.*
Limited by edition size of 10,394.
Issue price: $125.00

84-23-3.3
1974 *Riding to Hunt.*
Limited by edition size of 10,751.
Issue price: $150.00

84-23-3.4
1975 *Skating on the Brandywine.*
Limited by edition size of 8,058.
Issue price: $175.00

84-23-3.5
1976 *Brandywine Battlefield.*
Issue price: $180.00

UNITED STATES
GORHAM (Providence, Rhode Island)

84-27-1.1

In 1831, Jabez Gorham, a silversmith, established what is now Gorham Corporation, one of the world's largest producers of sterling silver. The firm manufactures flat silver and holloware, trophies, figurines, and ornaments. In 1885, a separate department was formed to make religious objects of silver, gold, and other materials. Gorham Corporation acquired crystal and china manufacturing companies in 1970, enabling it to produce limited-edition plates in china as well as in silver.

The *Rockwell Four Seasons* series which began in 1971, is an issue of four plates (Summer, Fall, Winter, and Spring) each year for 16 years. The *Remington* set of four plates, with artwork by Frederic Remington, was issued in 1973. A Christmas series with artwork by Norman Rockwell was begun in 1974. An annual series with artwork by Irene Spencer began in 1975.

All plates listed are made in china and trimmed in 24k gold. Limited by year of issue. Not Numbered.

Rockwell Four Seasons Series

Diameter: 10½ inches. Edition size undisclosed. Artist's signature appears on front of plate.

84-27-1.1
1971 *A Boy and His Dog.*
Issue price: $60.00

84-27-1.1

84-27-1.1

84-27-1.1

84-27-1.2
1972 *Young Love.*
Issue price: $60.00

84-27-1.2

84-27-1.2

84-27-1.2

84-27-1.3

UNITED STATES
GORHAM

84-27-1.3
1973 *The Ages of Love.*
Issue price: $60.00

84-27-1.3

84-27-1.3

84-27-1.3

84-27-1.4
1974 *Grandpa and Me.*
Issue price: $60.00

84-27-1.4

84-27-1.4

84-27-1.4

84-27-1.5
1975 *Me and My Pal.*
Issue price: $70.00

84-27-1.5

84-27-1.5

84-27-1.5

UNITED STATES
GORHAM

84-27-1.6

84-27-1.6
1976 *Grand Pals.*
Issue price: $70.00

84-27-1.6

84-27-1.6

84-27-1.6

Remington Plates

Diameter: 13½ inches. Editon size undisclosed. Artist's signature appears on front of plate.

84-27-2.1
1973 *The Old West.*
Issue price: $100.00

84-27-2.1

84-27-2.1

UNITED STATES
GORHAM

84-27-2.1

84-27-2.1

Rockwell Christmas Series

Diameter: 8½ inches. Edition size undisclosed. Artist's signature appears on front of plate.

84-27-3.1
1974 *Tiny Tim.*
Issue price: $12.50

84-27-3.2
1975 *Good Deeds.*
Issue price: $17.50

84-27-3.3
1976 *Christmas Trio.*
Issue price: $19.50

Irene Spencer Annual

Diameter: 8½ inches. Limited by announced edition size of 10,000. Artists signature appears on back of plate.

84-27-4.1
1975 *Dear Child.*
Issue price: $37.50

84-27-4.2
1976 *Promises to Keep.*
Issue price: $40.00

UNITED STATES
INTERNATIONAL (Meriden, Connecticut)

84-34-1.1

International Silver Company is one of the world's largest manufacturers of silver and silver-plated ware. The firm traces its origin to a pewter shop established by Ashbil Griswold in Meriden in 1808. Rogers Brothers, developers of an electroplating process, became affiliated with the firm in 1862. International Silver was incorporated in 1898. Limited-edition pewter plates were introduced in 1972 with the six-plate United States Bicentennial *We Are One* series. The Christmas series began in 1974; the *Presidential* series in 1975.

All plates listed are made in heavy-weight pewter (each plate weighing approximately 2 pounds) with sculpted designs in high relief. Ring provided for hanging. Numbered with certificate. Sculptor's name appears on back of plate.

Bicentennial Series

Diameter: 8¾ inches. Limited by edition size of 7,500. Artist: Manuel de Oliveiro; sculptor, Beverly Chase.

84-34-1.1
1972 *Declaration of Independence.*
Issue price: $40.00

84-34-1.2
1973 *The Midnight Ride of Paul Revere.*
Issue price: $40.00

84-34-1.3
1973 *Stand at Concord Bridge.*
Issue price: $40.00

84-34-1.4
1974 *Crossing the Delaware.*
Issue price: $50.00

84-34-1.5
1974 *Battle of Valley Forge.*
Issue price: $50.00

84-34-1.6
1975 *Surrender at Yorktown.*
Issue price: $50.00

Christmas Series

Diameter: 9-3/8 inches. Limited by edition size of 7,500.

84-34-2.1
1974 *Tiny Tim.*
Sculptor: Carl Sunberg. Issue price: $75.00

84-34-2.2

UNITED STATES
INTERNATIONAL

84-34-2.2
1975 *Caught.*
Artist: Thomas Nast; sculptor, Beverly Chase.
Issue price: $75.00

Presidential Series

Diameter: 9-3/4 inches. Limited by edition size of 7,500. Numbered with certificate. Sculptor: Beverly Chase.

84-34-3.1
1975 *The Inauguration of George Washington.*
Issue price: $75.00

UNITED STATES
LAKE SHORE PRINTS (Chicago, Illinois)

84-46-1.1

Plates issued by Lake Shore Prints are manufactured by two American companies, Gorham and Ridgewood. The *Rockwell Series* began in 1973 with artwork by Norman Rockwell. All plates listed are made in china.

Lake Shore Prints, Inc.

Rockwell Series

84-46-1.1
1973 *Butter Girl.*
Limited by announced edition size of 9,433.
Issue price: $14.95

84-46-1.2
1974 *The Truth About Santa.*
Limited by announced edition size of 15,141.
Issue price: $19.50

84-46-1.3
1975 *Home From the Fields.*
Limited by announced edition size of 8,500.
Issue price: $24.50

84-46-1.4
1976 *A President's Wife.*
Limited by announced edition size of 2,500.
Issue price: $70.00

84-50-1.1
LENOX (Pomona, New Jersey)

UNITED STATES

Walter Scott Lenox and his partner Jonathan Coxon, Sr. established the Ceramic Art Co. pottery in Trenton, New Jersey, in 1889. Lenox bought out Coxon in 1895 and operated the business alone until it was reorganized in 1906 as Lenox, Inc. The firm's early products were bowls, vases, and figurines in imitation of Irish Belleek. Later, tableware was added and during World War I Lenox was commissioned to supply President Wilson with dinner service — the first wholly American china ever used in The White House. The plant was later moved to Pomona.

In 1970, Lenox introduced its *American Bird* series of plates using the paintings of Edward Marshall Boehm. In 1973, the *Boehm Woodland Wildlife* series began with artwork adapted from original Boehm sculptures. All plates listed are hand-crafted in china with 25k gold decoration. Diameter: 10½ inches. Limited by announced edition size of 5,000. Not numbered. Artist's name appears on back of plate.

Two other plates based on Boehm bird paintings were issued, one in 1972 and one in 1973. These plates are made in bone china with an intaglio border filled with gold. Diameter: 13 inches. Not numbered. Artist's signature appears on front of plate.

LENOX

American Bird Series

84-50-1.1
1970 *Wood Thrush.*
Issue price: $35.00

84-50-1.2
1971 *Goldfinch.*
Issue price: $35.00

84-50-1.3
1972 *Mountain Bluebird.*
Issue price: $37.50

84-50-1.4
1973 *Meadowlark.*
Issue price: $50.00

84-50-1.5
1974 *Rufous Hummingbird.*
Issue price: $45.00

84-50-1.6
1975 *American Redstart.*
Issue price: $50.00

UNITED STATES
LENOX

84-50-2.1

Boehm Birds

84-50-2.1
1972 *The Bird of Peace* (Mute Swan).
Limited by announced edition size of 5,000.
Issue price: $150.00

84-50-2.2
1973 *Young America, 1776* (Eaglet).
Limited by announced edition size of 6,000.
Issue price: $175.00

Boehm Woodland Wildlife Series

84-50-3.1
1973 *Raccoons.*
Artist: Edward Marshall Boehm. Issue price: $50.00

84-50-3.2
1974 *Red Fox.*
Artist: Edward Marshall Boehm. Issue price: $52.50

84-50-3.3
1975 *Rabbits.*
Artist: Edward Marshall Boehm. Issue price: $58.50

84-60-1.1
PICKARD (Antioch, Illinois)

UNITED STATES

Pickard, Inc. was established in Chicago in 1897 by Wilder Austin Pickard. For some 40 years the Pickard China Studio (the firm's original name) was a decorating company, obtaining white blanks of bowls, pitchers, and other items from china factories in Europe and the United States. Pickard employed more than 50 artists to hand-paint and decorate the blanks. The firm was incorporated in 1925. Pickard established the present factory in Antioch in the 1930s to make his own china, chiefly tableware. In 1970, the firm introduced its series of limited-edition plates of American wildlife, painted by artist James Lockhart. During the first four years of the series the plates were issued in pairs. From 1974, individual plates were issued.

All plates listed are made in china with 23k gold design on the border. Numbered with certificate. Artist's signature appears on front of plate.

Lockhart Wildlife Series

84-60-1.1
1970 *Woodcock*
(pair) Diameter: 10½ inches. Limited by edition size of 2,000. Issue price: $150.00

84-60-1.1
1970 *Ruffed Grouse.*

84-60-1.2
1971 *Green-winged Teal*
(pair) Diameter: 10½ inches. Limited by edition size of 2,000. Issue price: $150.00

84-60-1.2
1971 *Mallard.*

84-60-1.3
1972 *Mockingbird*
(pair) Diameter: 10½ inches. Limited by edition size of 2,000. Issue price: $162.50

84-60-1.3
1972 *Cardinal.*

84-60-1.4
1973 *Wild Turkey*
(pair). Diameter: 10½ inches. Limited by edition size of 2,000. Issue price: $162.50

84-60-1.4
1973 *Ring-Necked Pheasant.*

UNITED STATES
PICKARD

84-60-1.5

84-60-1.5
1974 *American Bald Eagle.*
Diameter: 13 inches. Limited by edition size of 2,000. Issue price: $150.00

84-60-1.6
1975 *White-tailed Deer.*
Diameter: 11 inches. Limited by edition size of 2,500. Issue price: $100.00

84-66-1.1
REED & BARTON (Taunton, Massachusetts)

UNITED STATES

Reed & Barton Silversmiths traces its origin to a factory established by Isaac Babbitt in the early nineteenth century. In 1824, Babbitt developed an alloy, harder and more lustrous than pewter, which he named Britannia Metal. Henry G. Reed and Charles E. Barton, artists working for Babbitt, acquired the firm in the 1830s and continued to manufacture Britannia ware. In the late 1840s, the factory began to produce plated silverware. Reed & Barton was incorporated in 1888 and started producing solid silver services. Sterling flatware and holloware soon replaced plated ware as their largest line. In 1903, the firm began reproducing colonial pewter ware.

Reed & Barton began two limited-edition annual plate series in 1970: the *Bird* series based on artwork of John James Audubon, and the Christmas series. Since 1973, artwork for the Christmas plates has been based on old paintings.

All plates listed are hand-crafted in Damascene silver (an electroplating process patented by Reed & Barton). Diameter: 11 inches. Numbered without certificate.

Audubon Bird Series
Limited by edition size of 5,000.

84-66-1.1
1970 *Pine Siskin.*
Issue price: $60.00

84-66-1.2
1971 *Red-shouldered Hawk.*
Issue price: $60.00

84-66-1.3
1972 *Stilt Sandpiper.*
Issue price: $60.00

84-66-1.4
1973 *Red Cardinal.*
Issue price: $60.00

84-66-1.5
1974 *Boreal Chickadee.*
Issue price: $60.00

84-66-1.6
1975 *Yellow Breasted Chat.*
Issue price: $65.00

84-66-1.7
1976 *Bay-Breasted Warbler.*
Issue price: $65.00

UNITED STATES
REED & BARTON

84-66-2.1

Christmas Series

84-66-2.1
1970 *A Partridge in a Pear Tree.*
Artist: Robert Johnson. Limited by edition size of 2,500. Issue price: $55.00

84-66-2.2
1971 *We Three Kings of Orient Are.*
Artist: Robert Johnson. Limited by edition size of 7,500. Issue price: $60.00

84-66-2.3
1972 *Hark! The Herald Angels Sing.*
Artist: Robert Johnson. Limited by edition size of 7,500. Issue price: $60.00

84-66-2.4
1973 *Adoration of the Kings.*
Artwork based on painting by Rogier van der Weyden. Limited by edition size of 7,500. Issue price: $60.00

84-66-2.5
1974 *The Adoration of the Magi.*
Artwork based on 14th century Renaissance painting by Fra Angelice and Fra Lippi. Limited by edition size of 7,500. Issue price: $65.00

84-66-2.6
1975 *Adoration of the Kings.*
Artwork based on 15th century painting by Steven Lochner. Limited by edition size of 7,500. Issue price: $65.00

84-70-1.1
ROCKWELL SOCIETY (Slatersville, Rhode Island)

UNITED STATES

The Rockwell Society of America is a chartered organization devoted to the study of the works of Norman Rockwell. The Society began its Christmas series of previously unpublished Rockwells in 1974. The first issue was manufactured by Ridgewood. The second in the series was manufactured by the Edwin M. Knowles China Co. The Mother's Day series, also manufactured by Edwin M. Knowles began in 1976.

All plates listed are made in china. Diameter: 8¼ inches. Back hanger attached. Limited by announced period of issue. Edition size undisclosed. Numbered with certificate.

Christmas Series

84-70-1.1
1974 *Scotty Gets His Tree.*
Issue price: $24.50

84-70-1.2
1975 *Angel with a Black Eye.*
Issue price: $24.50

Mother's Day Series

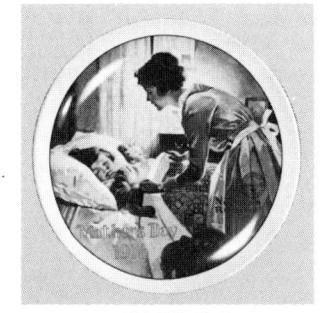

84-70-2.1
1976 *A Mother's Love.*
Issue price: $24.50

UNITED STATES
ROYAL DEVON (Providence, Rhode Island)

84-74-1.1

Royal Devon plates are manufactured by the Gorham Co. (see United States, GORHAM). The Christmas series and Mother's Day series both began in 1975. The artwork is by Norman Rockwell. All plates listed are made in china. Diameter: 8½ inches. Limited by year of issue. Edition size undisclosed. Not numbered. Artist's name appears on front of plate.

Christmas Series

84-74-1.1
1975 *Downhill Daring.*
Issue price: $24.50

Mother's Day Series

84-74-2.1
1975 *Doctor and the Doll.*
Issue price: $23.50

84-74-2.2
1976 *Puppy Love.*
Issue price: $24.50

84-78-1.1
ROYAL WORCESTER (Hudson, Massachusetts)

UNITED STATES

Royal Worcester U.S.A. is the American subsidiary of the English company of the same name (see England, ROYAL WORCESTER). The firm was established in New York after World War II. All plates in the following series are produced in the United States. In 1972, Royal Worcester initiated the *Birth of the Nation* series of five annual pewter plates to commemorate the Bicentennial of The United States. In 1974, the firm introduced its annual pewter plate series with artwork by Currier & Ives portraying life in mid-19th century America. The sculptor for both series is Prescott Baston.

All plates listed are made in solid pewter with designs in bas-relief. Limited by edition size of 10,000. Numbered without certificate.

Bicentennial Series
Diameter: 10¼ inches.

84-78-1.1
1972 *Boston Tea Party.*
Issue price: $45.00

84-78-1.2
1973 *The Ride of Paul Revere.*
Issue price: $45.00

84-78-1.3
1974 *Incident at Concord Bridge.*
Issue price: $50.00

84-78-1.4
1975 *Signing of the Declaration of Independence.*
Issue price: $65.00

84-78-1.5
1976 *Washington Crossing the Delaware.*
Issue price: $65.00

Currier & Ives Series
Diameter: 8 inches.

84-78-2.1
1974 *The Road — Winter.*
Issue price: $59.50

84-78-2.2
1975 *The Old Grist Mill.*
Issue price: $59.50

UNITED STATES
VERNONWARE (Manhattan Beach, California)

84-84-1.1

Vernonware is a subsidiary of Metlox Potteries. The factory, formerly called Vernon Kilns, was purchased by Metlox in 1958. Before 1971, the factory was known primarily for its fine dinnerware. In 1971, the Christmas plate series *Songs of Christmas* was begun. The plate borders are sculpted in the style of the 15th-century Florentine artist Della Robbia. Designs are by staff artists.

All plates listed are hand-crafted in earthenware with bas-relief border and are hand-painted. Diameter: 8½ inches. Limited by year of issue. Edition size undisclosed. Not numbered.

Christmas Series

84-84-1.1
1971 *A Partridge in a Pear Tree.*
Issue price: $15.00

84-84-1.2
1972 *Jingle Bells.*
Issue price: $15.00

84-84-1.3
1973 *The First Noel.*
Issue price: $15.00

84-84-1.4
1974 *It Came Upon a Midnight Clear.*
Issue price: $20.00

84-84-1.5
1975 *O Holy Night.*
Issue price: $20.00

Maker had no photo at presstime

84-84-1.6
1976 *Hark! The Herald Angels Sing.*
Issue price: $20.00

GLOSSARY OF COMMONLY USED TERMS

AFTERMARKET See MARKET.

ALABASTER A dense, fine-grained form of gypsum (calcium sulfate) stone, usually white to pink and slightly translucent. Alabaster stone can be carved in fine detail for ornamental objects and hardened by intense heat. Italian alabaster is also called Florentine marble. Ivory alabaster is composed of alabaster but is non-translucent and acquires a patina with age like that of old ivory.

ALLOTMENT A number of plates, all alike and usually at issue, allocated by a maker to a distributor or dealer. See LOT.

ALLOY Two metals combined while molten. Alloying is done to achieve hardness, toughness, or luster. See PEWTER.

ANNUAL A plate issued once each year as part of a series. The term is most often used when a plate does not commemorate a specific holiday.

ANNULAR KILN A round oven made from brick used to fire ceramic plates.

ART DECO, ART DECORATIF A style of decoration popular in Europe and America from 1920 to 1945. The Art Deco movement sought to glorify progress and the future by using as motifs such shapes as the cylinder, circle, rectangle, and cone.

ART NOUVEAU A style of decoration in Europe and America from 1890 to 1920. The Art Nouveau movement used twisting vegetable forms as its primary decorative motifs.

AT ISSUE A plate being offered for sale at the time of its manufacture and at the original price set by the maker.

BACKSTAMP The information on the back of a plate, usually including the maker's signature or name (logotype). It may also record serial number, title, artist's signature, explanation of the plate, sponsor, production techniques, awards, or release initials. It may be stamped, incised (cut or pressed), or applied as a decalcomania.

BAROQUE An elaborate style of decoration developed in Europe in the 17th and 18th Centuries and noted for exaggerated gesture and line. Example: Dresden plates (22-15-0.0).

BAS-RELIEF See RELIEF SCULPTURE.

BAVARIA A province in the southwest corner of Germany long known as a center for porcelain factories. The region contains large deposits of kaolin, the key porcelain component.

BEDROOM DEALER A trade term for a small dealer who usually operates from his home, buys discounted plates and resells them for a small profit.

BISQUE, BISCUIT A plate that has been fired but not glazed, leaving it with a matte texture. So called because of the biscuit-like appearance. Example: Lladro plates (72-46-0.0).

BLUE CHIP An established series by a well-known maker in which nearly every issue shows a steady sequence of price rises above issue price.

BODY 1. The formula or combination of substances that make up potter's clay, generally referring to stoneware and earthenware. 2. The basic plate form to which ornamentation is applied.

BONE ASH Calcium phosphate, a component of bone china, added to give whiteness and translucency. It is obtained by calcinating (reducing to powder by heat) animal bones, usually those of oxen.

BONE CHINA (BONE PORCELAIN) A type of china developed by Josiah Spode in England in the 1790s. By replacing part of the kaolin in the china formula with bone ash greater translucency and whiteness is obtained at lower firing temperatures. The finest bone china contains up to 50% bone ash. It is the most commonly made china in England. Examples: Royal Doulton (26-69-0.0), Royal Worcester, England (26-78-0.0) plates.

BULLISH Marked by rising prices, either actual or expected, and optimistic atmosphere. A *bull market* is one of rising prices.

BUY-ORDER A bid offered by an individual or dealer to purchase one or more plates of the same edition on the secondary market. See EXCHANGE.

CAMEO EFFECT Ornamentation in relief on a background of contrasting color to resemble a cameo. Example: Wedgwood Jasperware plates (26-90-0.0).

CELSIUS, CENTIGRADE The thermometric scale in which 0° represents the freezing point of water and 100° the boiling point. Celsius temperature is denoted by "C" after the number.

CERAMIC A general term applying to all of the various plates made from clay and hardened by firing.

CERTIFICATE An attestation of authenticity which may accompany each plate in an edition. A certificate authenticates a plate as being part of an issue and usually confirms the plate's individual number within the edition.

CHINA, CHINAWARE A hard, vitreous ceramic whose main components are kaolin and china stone fired at high temperature. Originally the term was used for these ceramics which only came from China. Later it was applied to all "hard" and "soft" *porcelain*. China is often used as a generic term which includes *porcelain* but is properly distinguished from it by a high bisque firing temperature and a low glaze firing temperature. The main firing (bisque) of china is approximately 7% lower than the main firing (glaze) of *porcelain*. In china production, the glaze is applied after the main firing and fixed with a second lower-temperature firing. A typical china formula is 40% kaolin, 10% ball clay, and varying proportions of china stone, feldspar, and flint. See PORCELAIN.

CHINA CLAY See KAOLIN.

CHINA STONE, PETUNTSE A feldspathic material in china formulas. China stone acts as a flux which helps dissolve and fuse the other components into a vitreous mass.

CHRISTMAS PLATES, CHRISTMAS SERIES Annual plates issued to commemorate Christmas, usually as part of a series. Plate names for Christmas include Noel (France), Weinachten (German), Jul (Danish), Navidad (Spanish and Portugese), and Natale (Italian). The oldest Christmas series is that of Bing & Grondahl, produced continuously since 1895 **(14-8-1.0)**.

CLAY Any of various plastic, viscous earths used to make plates. It is formed by the decomposition, due to weathering, of igneous rocks such as granite, feldspar, and pegmatite.

CLOSED-END SERIES A series of plates with a pre-determined number of issues. Example: Haviland *Twelve Days of Christmas* series **(18-30-1.0)**. See OPEN-END SERIES.

COBALT BLUE Cobalt oxide in the form of a dark black powder which, when fired, turns a deep blue. It was the first known and is still the most commonly used ceramic underglaze color because of its ability to withstand high firing temperatures. It can produce a variety of shades. Examples: Kaiser cobalt blue **(22-42-0.0)**, Bing & Grondahl Copenhagen blue **(14-8-0.0)**, Royal Copenhagen Danish blue **14-69-0.0)**, Rorstrand Scandia blue **(76-69-0.0)**.

COLLECTOR'S PLATE A decorative plate produced in a limited edition for the purpose of being collected. Although the earliest plates were not produced with this objective, they have since acquired the name by virtue of being collected and are now produced for this purpose.

COMMEMORATIVE PLATE A plate produced in rememberance of an event. Example: D'Arceau-Limoges *Lafayette Legacy* **(18-15-1.0)**.

COTERIE PLATE A collector's plate with a limited following whose trading is too infrequent to be listed on the Exchange but which may be traded over the counter.

CRYSTAL See LEAD CRYSTAL.

CUT GLASS Glass decorated by the cutting of grooves and facets, usually done with a copper engraver's wheel.

DAMASCENE An electro-plating effect created and patented by Reed & Barton **(88-66-0.0)** of etching and then depositing layers of copper and silver on bronze. Originally the term referred to the art, developed in Damascus, of ornamenting iron or steel with inlaid precious metals.

DEALER A marketer of plates who buys primarily from makers or distributors and sells primarily to the public.

DELFTWARE Earthenware covered with an opaque white glaze made of stannic oxide, an oxide of tin. Originally developed in Delft, Holland, in the 16th Century, Delftware has the appearance of being covered with a thick white paint. Similar ware is the *Majolica* of Italy and *Faience* of France and Germany. See FAIENCE, MAJOLICA.

DISTRIBUTOR A marketer of plates who buys from manufacturers and sells to dealers. Some distributors also act as makers and as dealers.

DRESDEN, MEISSEN Nearby cities in eastern Germany where the first hard-paste porcelain outside of china was produced by Johann Fredrich Bottger in 1708.

EARTHENWARE A term for any ceramics which are not vitrified. Typical components of earthenware are 43% ball clay, 24% kaolin, 23% flint, and 10% pegmatite. Fired earthenware is normally covered with either a transparent or opaque glaze. *High-fired earthenware* is fired at a higher temperature to produce a harder ware. Example: Royal Doulton Christmas plates **(26-69-1.0)**.

EDITION The total number of plates all with the same decoration, produced by a maker. Editions of collector's plates are normally limited to a fixed number and are not repeated.

ELECTRO-PLATING A process by which metal plates are coated with another metal by electrical charges.

EMBOSSED DESIGN Raised ornamentation produced by the plate mold or by stamping a design into the body of a plate. Example: Belleek plates **(34-8-0.0)**.

ENAMEL A glaze material colored with suspended mineral oxides for decorating plates.

ENGRAVED DESIGN Decoration produced by cutting into the surface of metal, glass, or china plates with either a tool or acid, as in etching. Example: Veneto Flair plates **(38-84-0.0)**.

ETCHED DESIGN Decoration produced by cutting into the surface of a plate with acid. The plate is first covered with an acid-resistant paint or wax, and the design is carved through this coating. When the plate is immersed, the acid "bites" into the plate surface in the shape of the design. Example: Franklin Mint silver plates **(84-23-0.0)**.

EXCHANGE A place where plates are traded, most commonly the Bradford Exchange, the largest trading center. Incorporated in 1962, it was formerly known as Bradford Galleries Exchange.

FAIENCE Tin-enameled earthenware from France, Germany, or Spain developed in the 17th Century and named for the Italian town of Faenza, a center for *Majolica*, another name for this ware. See DELFTWARE.

FELDSPAR A mineral composed of aluminum silicates with either potassium, sodium, calcium, or barium. Feldspar decomposes to form kaolin, the key ingredient of china and porcelain. The addition of undecomposed feldspar to china formulas gives the ware greater hardness.

FIRE The heating process which hardens ceramic plates in a kiln. Ceramic clay begins to undergo chemical change at 500° C and vitrifies around 1300° C.

FIRST EDITION The first, and presumably the only, edition of a collector's plate. The term (or its abbreviation "FE") is sometimes used for the edition which is the *first issue* in a series of collector' plates. However, since no edition is normally ever reopened and therefore no "second edition" is possible, all issues of collector's plates are properly termed first editions.

FIRST ISSUE Chronologically, the first plate in a series, i.e., the plates issued in the first year of an annual series.

FLUX Finely ground material added to porcelain formulas which lowers the vitrification temperature and helps fuse the components. Example: Feldspar.

GLAZE Glassy, hard surface coating on plates made of silicates (glass-forming compounds) and mineral oxides. Glaze is put on ceramic ware to make it wear-

GLOSSARY OF COMMONLY USED TERMS

resistant, waterproof, decorative, and to seal the pores. Glaze material suspended in water is applied after the first firing and is heated to the glaze's vitrification point when it fuses to the plate body. Glaze is applied by dipping, spraying, or painting. Decorating is added under, over, or with the glaze layer. See UNDERGLAZE.

INTAGLIO Decoration created by cutting beneath the surface of the plate. See ENGRAVED DESIGN or ETCHED DESIGN.

INCISED DESIGN Ornamentation cut into the body of the plate.

IRIDESCENCE A rainbow effect on a plate's surface caused by the diffraction of light. True iridescent color effects are readily distinguished from a plate's inherent color because the pattern will change as the plate is moved. Example: Belleek plates **(34-8-0.0)**.

ISSUE 1. The release for sale of an edition of plates by a maker. 2. A plate in an edition. 3. An edition within a series.

ISSUE PRICE Original or first price of plate established by the maker at the time the plate is released for sale.

JASPERWARE Hard, fine-grained, unglazed stoneware made by adding barium sulfate to clay, developed by Josiah Wedgwood in the 1770s. The term "jasper" does not indicate the presence of jasper stone but most likely denotes the varieties of colors in which Jasperware can be produced. Though white in its original form, Jasperware can be stained in blue, green, lilac, yellow, maroon, or black to serve as a background for embossments of white Jasper relief for a cameo effect. When stained throughout the body it is called *solid Jasperware*. Example: Wedgwood plates **(26-90-0.0)**.

KAOLIN The only clay which yields a white material when fired and the indispensable element of porcelain and china plates. Also called *true clay* or *china clay*, it is formed by the complete decomposition by weathering of feldspar. Kaolin is a refractory clay which can be fired at high temperatures without deforming. It produces a vitreous, translucent ceramic when fired with fluxes (fusible rocks) such as feldspar. The components of kaolin clay are 50% silica, 33% alumina, 2% oxides, 1% magnesia, 2% alkali, and 12% water.

LEAD CRYSTAL Extremely transparent fine quality glass, also called *flint glass* and *lead glass*, which contains a high proportion of lead oxide to give extra weight, better refractiveness, and a clear ringing tone when tapped. *Full lead crystal* identifies glass with a 24% or greater lead content. Examples: Crystal D'Albret **(18-12-0.0)** and Lalique **(18-46-0.0)** plates.

LIMITED-EDITION PLATES Plates produced in a fixed quantity, either predetermined or determined by a specific period of production. All true collector's plates are in limited editions.

LIMOGES A town in south central France famous for its porcelain production because of the discovering of nearby kaolin deposits in 1768. Limoges porcelain manufacturers have joined together to enforce quality standards. Examples: D'Arceau-Limoges **(18-15-0.0)**, Haviland **(18-30-0.0)** and Haviland-Parlon **(18-32-0.0)**.

LISTED PLATE A plate listed and regularly quoted on the Bradford Exchange. See OVER THE COUNTER PLATE.

LOT A number of plates, all in the same edition and represented by a sell-order on the Exchange, usually on the secondary market and not at issue. See ALLOTMENT.

LUSTRE Decoration applied to a plate surface by application of metallic oxides such as gold, silver, platinum, or copper over the glaze. When gently fired, this leaves a thin metallic film.

MAJOLICA, MAIOLICA Earthenware finished with opaque white enamel, similar to *Faience* and *Delftware*, but first made in the Spanish island of Majorca.

MAKER The name by which a plate is known or under which it is issued, i.e., manufacturer, distributor or sponsor. In most cases the "maker" is the actual manufacturer, i.e., Bing and Grondahl **(14-8-0.0)**. However, it can also be a commissioner or distributor, i.e., Schmid **(22-85-0.0)**, using a trade name, while the physical production is in fact done by a sub-contractor.

MARKET The structure within which plates are bought and sold. The *primary market* consists of new issues which are sold by the makers or their sales representatives to dealers to distributors. Dealers and distributors in turn normally sell the new issues to the public at issue price. The *secondary market* or *aftermarket* is the buying and selling of plates previously sold, and usually sold out, on the primary market. In many cases secondary market prices are higher than those of the primary market before a plate edition is sold out.

MARKET BRADEX A kind of "Dow Jones" index of the overall collector's plate market expressed as a percentage, determined by the current price/issue ratio of 12 key series.

MARKET PRICE The price at which a plate is currently traded regardless of its issue price. See ISSUE PRICE.

MEISSEN See DRESDEN.

MINT CONDITION A plate in new or like-new condition accompanied by any original certificates and packing materials included at issue.

MODELING The process of making the original pattern from which the master mold is made for a sculptured plate.

MOLD A general term for the form which gives a plate its shape. Clay, metal, or glass is pressed into a mold to form a *blank* (without ornamentation). Intaglio decoration or raised ornamentation may also be formed in the mold. China or porcelain *slip-casting* is done in plaster of paris molds. Slip (diluted clay formula) is poured into the mold, and the excess water is absorbed into the plaster of paris.

OPEN-END SERIES A continuing series of annual plates with no established termination. Example: Royal Copenhagen Christmas series **(14-69-0.0)**. See CLOSED-END SERIES.

OPEN STOCK Plates available in or produced in unlimited numbers or for an unlimited time period (and therefore not considered collector's plates).

OVER THE COUNTER PLATE A collector's plate occassionally traded directly between specialized dealers but not listed on the Exchange and not normally traded through it. See LISTED PLATE.

OVERGLAZE DECORATION A design painted or printed on a plate after it has been glazed and fired. Overglaze decoration is then fixed by a light firing.

OVERLAY CRYSTAL Crystal plates produced by lay-

GLOSSARY OF COMMONLY USED TERMS

ing one layer of glass on another and fusing them while molten. Example: Royale Germania plates (28-81-0.0).

PASTE The combination of substances that make up potter's clay, generally that for porcelain or china.

PEWTER An alloy of tin with copper and antimony as hardeners. The greater the amount of copper and antimony, the harder the ware. *Fine pewter* is composed of 80% tin and 20% antimony and brass or copper. Examples: International (84-34-0.0) and Royal Worcester (U.S.A.) (84-78-0.0) plates. See ALLOY.

PORCELAIN The hardest vitreous ceramic fired at the highest temperatures. Although the term *porcelain* is often interchanged with *china,* true porcelain as the term is used in the field is distinguished from china by its very high glaze firing and low bisque firing temperature compared with the high bisque firing and low glaze firing of china. The main firing (glaze) of porcelain is approximately 7% higher than the main firing (bisque) of china. The glaze fuses with the porcelain plate body and produces an extremely hard surface. *Hard-paste* or *true porcelain* is made from a formula whose primary components are kaolin and china stone (petuntse). When fired, the china stone vitrifies, producing a hard, glassy ceramic. True porcelain is translucent when thin, white unless colored, impervious to scratching, and transmits a ringing tone when struck. A typical porcelain formula is 50% kaolin, 25% quartz, and 25% feldspar. *Soft-paste porcelain* was developed in Renaissance Europe in an attempt to imitate the true porcelain of China. Soft-paste porcelain was a mixture of white sand, gypsum, soda, alum, salt, and niter, fired until it vitrified. It had a soft texture, great sensitivity to sudden temperature changes, was warmer to the touch than true porcelain, and could be scratched with a file. The terms "hard" and "soft" porcelain refer to the "hard" firing (around 1450° C) temperature required for true porcelain and the "soft" firing (around 1150° C) temperature used for soft-paste porcelain. See CHINA.

POINT, BRADEX POINT One percentage point of the Market Bradex.

POTTERY 1. A general term used for all ceramic ware but strictly speaking for earthenware and non-vitrified ceramics. 2. The place or kilns where ceramic objects are fired.

RELIEF SCULPTURE Sculpture in which the design or figure is not free-standing but is raised from a background. There are three degrees of relief sculpture: *Alto-relievo* or high relief, where the design is almost detached from the background; *Basso-relievo* or bas-relief, where the design is raised somewhat; and *Relievo-stiacciato,* where the design is scarcely more than scratched. Relief designs on plates may be formed in the plate mold or formed separately and applied to the plate body.

SECOND, SECOND SORTING A plate judged to be a grade below first quality, usually indicated by a scratch or gouge through the glaze over the backstamp on the back.

SECONDARY MARKET See MARKET.

SELL ORDER An offer at an asked price given by an individual or dealer to sell one or more plates of the same edition on the secondary market, usually on the Exchange. See LOT.

SLIP Ceramic paste or body diluted with water to a smooth, creamy consistency used for *slip-casting.* See MOLD.

STEATITE, SOAPSTONE A natural rock whose primary component is talc. Steatite is used in porcelain formulas as a flux.

STERLING SILVER An alloy which, by United States law, must have the minimum fineness of 92.5% by weight of pure silver and a maximum of 7.5% by weight of a base metal, usually copper. Example: Franklin Mint plates (84-23-0.0).

STONEWARE A hard ceramic fired to vitrification but not to translucency. Typical components of stoneware are 30% ball clay, 32% kaolin, 15% flint, and 23% cornish stone. Example: Wedgwood's Jasperware plates (26-90-0.0).

SUPERMARKET PLATE Common term for a plate edition of dubious limitations, cheaply produced, and not considered a true collector's plate.

TERRA-COTTA A general term for any kind of fired clay. Strictly speaking, terra-cotta is an earthenware produced from a clay which fires to a dull ochre or red color. The ware, left unglazed, is coarse and porous. Example: Veneto Flair plates (38-84-0.0).

TIN GLAZE A glaze colored white by oxide of tin which produces a heavy, opaque surface when fired. See DELFTWARE.

TRANSLUCENT The qualify of transmitting light without transparence. In a plate, translucency depends on the quality of the china or porcelain, thickness of the plate, and firing temperature. Underfired porcelain is not translucent.

TRUE CLAY See KAOLIN.

UNDERGLAZE DECORATION Decoration applied after a plate has been fired once (bisque fired) but before it is glazed and fired a second time. Underglaze painting is most commonly done in cobalt blue pigment (although other colors can be used) because this is the most stable color and can withstand high firing temperatures. *"True underglaze technique"* means such painting was done by hand.

VITRIFICATION A fusion of potters clay at temperatures between 1250° C and 1450° C, to form a glassy, nonporous substance. With continued heating, the substance will become translucent.

INDEXES

A-6
INDEX OF PLATE MAKERS AND SPONSORS

NOTE: "Maker" is a general term for the name under which a plate is issued which is not necessarily the actual "manufacturer." A Maker can be a distributor, manufacturer, or occasionally a "sponsor." See GLOSSARY OF COMMONLY USED TERMS.

Anri	**38-4-0.0**
L'Association L'Esprit de Lafayette	See D'Arceau-Limoges
B & G	See Bing & Grondahl
Bareuther	**22-6-0.0**
Belleek	**34-8-0.0**
Berlin	**22-8-0.0**
Beswick, John Potteries	See Royal Doulton
Bing & Grondahl	**14-8-0.0**
Chambre Syndicale de la Couture Parisienne	See D'Arceau-Limoges
Creative World	See Veneto Flair
Cristal D'Albret	**18-12-0.0**
Cristalleries et Verreries de Vianne	See Cristal D'Albret
Danish Church	**22-13-0.0**
D'Arceau-Limoges	**18-15-0.0**
Desiree	See Svend Jensen
Dresden	**22-15-0.0**
Franklin Mint	**84-23-0.0**
Furstenberg	**22-23-0.0**
Goebel	**22-27-0.0**
Gorham	**84-27-0.0** See also Royal Devon
Haviland	**18-30-0.0**
Haviland Parlon	**18-32-0.0**
Hummelwerk	See Goebel
Hutte, Josephine	See Royale Germania
International	**84-34-0.0**
Georg Jensen	**14-38-0.0**
Svend Jensen	**14-40-0.0**
Kaiser	**32-42-0.0**
Kings	**38-43-0.0**
Knowles, Edwin M.	See Rockwell Society
Lafayette Society	See D'Arceau-Limoges
Lake Shore Prints	**84-46-0.0**
Lalique	**18-46-0.0**
Lanternier, A. et Cie.	See Royal Limoges
Lenox	**84-50-0.0**
Lihs-Lindner	**32-47-0.0**
Lladro	**72-46-0.0**
Metlox Potteries	See Vernonware
Orrefors	**76-57-0.0**
Pickard	**84-60-0.0**
Procelana Granada	**4-61-0.0**
Porsgrund	**54-61-0.0**
R.C.	See Royal Copenhagen
Reed & Barton	**84-66-0.0**
Ridgewood	See Lake Shore Prints, Rockwell Society
Rockwell Society of America	**84-70-0.0**
Rorstrand	**76-69-0.0**
Rosenthal	**22-69-0.0**
Royal Bayreuth	**22-73-0.0**
Royal Copenhagen	**14-69-0.0**
Royal Devon	**84-74-0.0**
Royal Doulton	**26-69-0.0**
Royal Limoges	**18-69-0.0**
Royal Tettau	See Royal Bayreuth
Royal Worcester	(G.B.) **26-78-0.0** (U.S.A.) **84-78-0.0**
Royale	**22-77-0.0**
Royale Germania	**22-81-0.0**
Sango	**42-72-0.0**
Santa-Clara	**72-72-0.0**
La Scala, Museo Teatrale alla Scala	See di Volteradici
Schmid	(Ger.) **22-85-0.0** (Jap.) **42-85-0.0**
Spode	**26-86-0.0**
Veneto Flair	**38-84-0.0**
Vernonware	**84-84-0.0**
di Volteradici	**38-72-0.0**
Wedgwood	**26-90-0.0**

INDEX OF PLATE SERIES BY TYPE AND NAME

ANNIVERSARY
Goebel *(Hummel)* 22-27-3.1
Kaiser . . . . 22-42-3.1 to 22-42-3.5

ANNUAL
Goebel *(Hummel)* . . . . 22-27-1.1 to 22-27-1.6
Lalique . . . . 18-46-1.1 to 18-46-1.12
Orrefors *(Cathedral)* . . . . 76-57-1.1 to 76-57-1.6
Royale Germania . . . . 22-81-1.1 to 22-81-1.6

AUDUBON
Reed & Barton . . . . 84-66-1.1 to 84-66-1.7

BELLINI
Veneto Flair 38-84-1.1

BICENTENNIAL
D'Arceau-Limoges . . . . 18-15-1.1 to 18-15-1.7
Haviland . . . . 18-30-2.1 to 18-30-2.5
International . . . . 84-34-1.1 to 84-34-1.6
Royal Copenhagen . . . . 14-69-3.1 to 14-69-3.2
Royal Worcester . . . . 84-78-1.1 to 84-78-1.5
Wedgwood . . . . 26-90-3.1 to 26-90-3.6

BIRDS
Lenox . . . . 84-50-1.1 to 84-50-1.5;
                                              84-50-2.1 to 84-50-2.2
Royal Worcester *(Doughty)* . . . . . . 26-78-1.1 to 26-78-1.5
Veneto Flair . . . . 38-84-4.1 to 38-84-4.3

CATS
Veneto Flair . . . . 38-84-10.1 to 38-84-10.3

CHRISTMAS
Anri . . . . 38-4-1.1 to 38-4-1.6
Bareuther . . . . 22-6-1.1 to 22-6-1.10
Belleek . . . . 34-8-1.1 to 34-8-1.6
Berlin . . . . 22-8-1.1 to 22-8-1.7
Bing & Grondahl *(Jubilee)* . . . . 14-8-1.1 to 14-8-1.82;
                                              14-8-2.1 to 14-8-2.13
D'Arceau-Limoges . . . . 18-15-2.1 to 18-15-2.2
Dresden . . . . 22-15-1.1 to 22-15-1.6
Franklin Mint . . . . 84-23-1.1 to 84-23-1.6
Furstenberg *(Deluxe Christmas)* . . 22-23-1.1 to 22-23-1.6;
                                              22-23-2.1 to 22-23-2.3
Georg Jensen . . . . 14-38-1.1 to 14-38-1.4
Gorham . . . . 84-27-3.1 to 84-27-3.3
Haviland . . . . 18-30-1.1 to 18-30-1.7
Haviland Parlon . . . . 18-32-2.1 to 18-32-2.4
International . . . . 84-34-2.1 to 84-34-2.2
Kaiser . . . . 22-42-1.1 to 22-42-1.7
Kings . . . . 38-43-1.1 to 38-43-1.4
Lihs-Lindner . . . . 22-47-1.1 to 22-47-1.5
Lladro . . . . 72-46-1.1 to 72-46-1.4
Porcelana Granada . . . . 4-61-1.1 to 4-61-1.6
Porsgrund . . . . 54-61-1.1 to 54-61-1.9
Reed & Barton . . . . 84-66-2.1 to 84-66-2.6
Rockwell Society . . . . 84-70-1.1 to 84-70-1.2
Rorstrand . . . . 76-69-1.1 to 76-69-1.8
Rosenthal

(Traditional, Wiinblad) . . . . 22-69-1.1 to 22-69-1.67;
                                              22-69-2.1 to 22-69-2.6
Royal Bayreuth . . . . 22-73-1.1 to 22-73-1.4
Royal Copenhagen . . . . 14-69-1.1 to 14-69-1.69
Royal Devon 84-74-1.1
Royal Doulton . . . . 26-69-1.1 to 26-69-1.5
Royal Limoges . . . . 18-69-1.1 to 18-69-1.2
Royale . . . . 22-77-1.1 to 22-77-1.8
Santa Clara . . . . 72-72-1.1 to 72-72-1.6
Schmid *(Peanuts, Disney)* . . . . 42-85-3.1 to 42-85-3.3;
                                              42-85-1.1 to 42-85-1.5
Schmid Hummel . . . . 22-85-1.1 to 22-85-1.6
Spode . . . . 26-86-1.1 to 26-86-1.6
Svend Jensen . . . . 14-40-1.1 to 14-40-1.6
Veneto Flair . . . . 38-84-2.1 to 38-84-2.4;
                                              38-84-11.1 to 38-84-11.2
Vernonware . . . . 84-84-1.1 to 84-84-1.6
Wedgwood . . . . 26-90-1.1 to 26-90-1.7

CHURCH
Danish Church . . . . 22-13-1.1 to 22-13-1.8
Orrefors . . . . 76-57-1.1 to 76-57-1.7

COLLECTOR'S INTERNATIONAL
Royal Doulton *(Commedia
  Dell 'Arte, Flower Garden,
  Ports of Call, Log of the
  Dashing Wave)* . . . . 26-69-3.1 to 26-69-3.2;
                                              26-69-4.1 to 26-69-4.2;
                                              26-69-5.1 to 26-69-5.2;
                                              26-69-6.1

COMMEDIA DELL 'ARTE
Royal Doulton . . . . 26-69-3.1 to 26-69-3.2

CURRIER & IVES
Royal Worcester . . . . 26-78-2.1 to 26-78-2.2

DISNEY
Schmid Bros. . . . . 42-85-3.1 to 42-85-3.4
                                              42-85-4.1 to 42-85-4.3

DOGS
Veneto Flair . . . . 38-84-5.1 to 38-84-5.5

EASTER
Furstenberg . . . . 22-23-3.1 to 22-23-3.6
Lihs Lindner . . . . 22-47-3.1 to 22-47-3.3
Porsgrund . . . . 54-61-4.1 to 54-61-4.5
Veneto Flair . . . . 38-84-8.1 to 38-84-8.4

FATHER'S DAY
Anri . . . . 38-4-2.1 to 38-4-2.4
Bareuther . . . . 22-6-2.1 to 22-6-2.8
Berlin . . . . 22-8-2.1 to 22-8-2.6
Porsgrund . . . . 54-61-3.1 to 54-61-3.6
Rorstrand . . . . 26-69-2.1 to 26-69-2.4
Royale . . . . 22-77-2.1 to 22-77-2.7

FLOWER GARDEN
Royal Doulton . . . . 26-69-4.1 to 26-69-4.2

INDEX OF PLATE SERIES BY TYPE AND NAME

FLOWERS
Kings..................38-43-2.1 to 38-43-2.4

FOUR SEASONS
Cristal D'Albert..........18-12-1.1 to 18-12-1.4
Gorham.................84-27-1.1 to 84-27-1.6

HUMMEL, BERTA
Goebel.................22-27-1.1 to 22-27-1.5
Schmid................22-85-1.1 to 22-85-1.6;
 22-85-2.1 to 22-85-2.5

IRENE SPENCER
Franklin Mint...........84-23-2.1 to 84-23-2.4
Gorham................84-27-4.1 to 84-27-4.6

JUBILEE
Bing & Grondahl.........14-8-2.1 to 14-8-2.13

LAST SUPPER
Veneto Flair............38-84-6.1 to 38-84-6.3

LIVING AMERICAN ARTISTS
Sango..................42-72-1.1

LOG OF THE DASHING WAVE
Royal Doulton...........26-69-6.1

MOSAIC
Veneto Flair............38-84-9.1 to 38-84-9.2

MOTHER'S DAY
Anri...................38-4-3.1 to 38-4-3.5
Bareuther..............22-6-3.1 to 22-6-3.8
Berlin.................22-8-3.1 to 22-8-3.6
Bing & Grondahl........14-8-3.1 to 14-8-3.8
Dresden...............22-15-2.1 to 22-15-2.5
Franklin Mint...........84-23-2.1 to 84-23-2.4
Furstenberg............22-23-4.1 to 22-23-4.5
Georg Jensen..........14-38-2.1 to 14-28-2.3
Goebel................22-27-4.1 to 22-27-4.2
Haviland..............18-30-3.1 to 18-30-3.4
Haviland Parlon........18-32-3.1 to 18-32-3.2
Kaiser................22-42-2.1 to 22-42-2.6
Kings.................38-43-3.1 to 38-43-3.4
Lihs Lindner...........22-47-2.1 to 22-47-2.4
Lladro................72-46-2.1 to 72-46-2.6
Orrefors..............76-57-2.1 to 76-57-2.6
Porsgrund.............54-61-2.1 to 54-61-2.7
Rockwell Society.......84-70-2.1
Rosenthal.............22-69-5.1
Rorstrand.............76-69-3.1 to 76-69-3.5
Royal Bayreuth........22-73-2.1 to 22-73-2.4
Royal Copenhagen.....14-69-2.1 to 14-69-2.6
Royal Devon..........84-74-2.1 to 84-74-2.2
Royal Doulton.........26-69-2.1 to 26-69-2.4
Royale Germania......22-81-2.1 to 22-81-2.5
Royale...............22-77-3.1 to 22-77-3.7
Sango................42-72-2.1
Schmid *(Disney, Peanuts)*......42-85-4.1 to 42-85-4.3;
 42-85-2.1 to 42-85-2.5
Schmid Hummel........22-85-2.1 to 22-85-2.5
Svend Jensen.........14-40-2.1 to 14-40-2.7
Veneto Flair..........38-84-7.1 to 38-84-7.5
Wedgwood...........26-90-2.1 to 26-90-2.6

NOBILITY OF CHILDREN
Rosenthal.............22-69-6.1

OPERA
Studio Dante di Volteradici....38-72-1.1

ORIENTAL NIGHTS
Rosenthal.............22-69-4.1

PEACE
Cristal D'Albert........18-12-2.1

PEANUTS
Schmid Bros..........42-85-1.1 to 42-85-1.5;
 42-85-2.1 to 42-85-2.5

PORTS OF CALL
Royal Doulton.........26-69-5.1 to 26-69-5.2

PRESIDENTIAL
International..........84-34-3.1

REMINGTON
Gorham..............84-27-2.1

ROCKWELL
Franklin Mint..........84-23-1.1 to 84-23-1.6
Gorham..............84-27-1.1 to 84-27-1.5
Lake Shore Prints.....84-46-1.1 to 84-46-1.3
Rockwell Society Christmas....84-70-1.1 to 84-70-1.2
Royal Devon.........84-74-1.1
Sango...............42-72-1.1

SUNBONNET BABIES
Royal Bayreuth.......22-73-3.1

TAPESTRY
Haviland Parlon......18-32-1.1 to 18-32-1.6

THANKSGIVING
Bareuther............22-6-4.1 to 22-6-4.6

TRESTER
Rosenthal............22-69-3.1

VALENTINE'S DAY
Royal Doulton........26-69-7.1

WILDLIFE
Goebel..............22-27-2.1 to 22-27-2.3
Lenox Boehm........84-50-3.1 to 84-50-3.3
Pickard Lockhart.....84-60-1.1 to 84-60-1.6
Veneto Flair.........38-84-3.1 to 38-84-3.4

WOMEN
D'Arceau-Limoges....18-15-3.1 to 18-15-3.2

WYETH
Franklin Mint.........84-23-3.1 to 84-23-3.5

A-9

INDEX OF PLATE TITLES

A

Aabenraa Market	14-69-1.14
Across the Delaware	26-90-3.4
Adoration of Christ	38-48-1.1
Adoration of the Kings	84-66-2.4; 84-66-2.6
The Adoration of the Magi	84-66-2.5
Advent Branch	22-69-1.13
The Ages of Love	84-27-1.3
Along the Brandywine	84-23-3.1
Alpine Christmas	38-4-1.6
Alpine Father and Children	38-4-2.1; 38-4-2.2
Alpine Mother and Children	38-4-3.1; 38-4-3.2; 38-4-3.3
Alpine Horn	38-4-1.3
Alpine Stroll	38-4-3.4
Amalienborg Palace, Copenhagen	4-69-1.47
American Bald Eagle	84-60-1.5
American Mother	14-69-2.1
American Redstart	84-50-1.6
Angel	38-84-2.4
Angel in a Christmas Setting	22-85-1.1
Angel of Peace	22-69-1.8
Angel with a Black Eye	84-70-1.2
Angel with Flute	22-85-1.2
Angel with Trumpet	22-69-2.6
The Annunciation	4-61-1.1
Anxiety of the Coming Christmas	14-8-1.11
Archangel	72-72-1.4
Arrival of the Christmas Boat	14-8-1.23
Arrival of Christmas Guests	14-8-1.43
Arrival of the Christmas Train	14-8-1.37
The Ascension	22-69-2.5
Autumn	18-12-1.2

B

Balloon	22-8-2.4
The Baptism of Achilles	26-90-2.3
Barn Owl	22-27-2.3
Basilica di San Marco	76-57-1.3
Basilica di San Pietro, Rome	76-57-1.6
The Battle of Brandywine	18-15-1.4
Battle of Concord	26-90-3.3
Battle of Valley Forge	84-34-1.5
Bay-Breasted Warbler	84-66-1.7
Bear and Cubs	14-8-3.6
Behind the Frozen Window	14-8-1.1; 14-8-2.1
Bell Tower of Old Church in Jutland	14-69-1.35
Berchtesgaden	22-69-1.28
Bird and Chicks	14-8-3.2; 72-46-2.2
Bird in Nest	14-69-2.5
Bird of Peace	18-12-2.1; 84-50-2.1
Birds	54-61-4.2
Birthplace of Hans Christian Andersen, with Snowman	14-8-1.60
Blackbird at Christmastime	14-69-1.59
Blackburnian Warbler	26-78-1.4
Bluebells	38-43-2.4
Blue-Grey Gnatcatchers	26-78-1.3
Blue Titmouse	22-27-2.2
Blue-Winged Sivas and Bamboo	26-78-1.5
Boeslunde Church, Zealand	14-69-1.43
Boreal Chickadee	84-66-1.5
Boston Tea Party	18-30-2.2; 26-90-3.1; 84-78-1.1
A Bouquet for Mother	14-40-2.1; 22-47-2.3
Boy and Dog on Christmas Eve	14-38-1.2
Boy and Geese	54-61-2.2
Boy and Girl	72-46-1.3
Boy and Goats	54-61-2.5
A Boy and His Dog	84-27-1.1
Brandywine Battlefield	84-23-3.5
Breakfast	18-30-3.1
Bringing Home the Christmas Tree	14-8-1.71; 22-42-1.6
Bringing Home the Tree	84-23-1.1; 76-69-1.1
Bringing Home the Yule Tree	14-8-1.19
Broager Kirken	22-13-1.7
Brooklyn Bridge on Opening Day	22-8-2.1
Building a Snowman	42-85-3.4
The Bumblebee	22-85-2.3
Bunnies	54-61-4.3
Burning of the Gaspee	18-30-2.1
Butter Girl	84-46-1.1

C

Camping	22-77-2.4
Candle Lighting	76-69-3.4
Canoeing down River	22-42-3.3
Carolers	72-46-1.2; 72-46-1.4; 84-23-1.3
Caroling	72-46-1.1; 42-85-3.3
Carriage in the Village	22-73-1.1
Castle Caldwell	34-8-1.1
The Castle of Cochen	22-69-1.67
Castle Heidelberg	22-6-2.3
Castle Hohenschwangau	22-6-2.4
Castle Hohenzollern	22-6-2.8
Castle Katz	22-6-2.5
Castle Lichtenstein	22-6-2.7
Castle Neuschwanstein	22-6-2.1
Castle Pfalz	22-6-2.2
Cat and Kittens	54-61-2.4; 14-8-3.3
Cats	22-42-2.3; 22-8-3.5; 22-27-4.2
Caught	84-34-2.2
The Celtic Cross	34-8-1.2; 34-8-1.6
Chained Dog Getting a Double Meal on Christmas Eve	14-8-1.21; 14-8-2.3
Chalet Christmas	22-69-1.19
Chapel in the Hills	22-6-1.10
Chapel in Oberndorf	22-6-1.4
Charlie Brown	42-85-2.1
Chase of the Unicorn	18-32-1.3
Cherubs	72-46-1.5
Chicks	22-23-3.2; 38-84-8.2; 54-61-4.4
A Child is Born in Bethlehem	54-61-1.4
Children and Puppy	76-57-2.6
Children in the Winter Woods	22-69-1.14
Children in the Woods	72-72-1.3
The Child's Christmas	14-8-1.31
The Chimney Sweep	14-40-1.5

INDEX OF PLATE TITLES

Christ 38-84-6.5
Christbaum 26-86-1.6
Christ Child 22-69-1.23; 38-84-2.3
Christ Church, Philadelphia 76-57-1.7
Christ the Saviour is Born 22-42-1.7
Christbaum 26-86-1.6
Christkindlesmarkt 22-6-1.3
Christmas Angel 14-69-1.44
Christmas at Home 14-8-1.77
Christmas at the Seaport 22-77-1.8
Christmas by the Sea 22-69-1.26; 22-69-1.48
Christmas Candles 14-8-1.63
Christmas Carolers 22-42-1.5
Christmas Celebration in Francone . 22-69-1.63
Christmas Cheer 22-47-1.4
Christmas Child 22-85-1.5
Christmas Damn 22-77-1.5
Christmas During War 22-69-1.7
The Christmas Elf 14-8-1.69
Christmas Eve 14-8-1.65; 22-23-1.3; 22-23-2.3; 22-69-1.45; 22-69-1.49; 22-69-1.53; 38-84-11.1
Christmas Eve at the Doghouse 42-85-1.2
Christmas Eve at the Fireplace 42-85-1.3
Christmas Eve in Augsburg 22-8-1.7
Christmas Eve in the Country 72-72-1.6
Christmas Fair in Ebeltoft 22-77-1.1
Christmas in an Alpine Valley 22-69-1.37
Christmas in a Small Village 22-69-1.51
Christmas in a Village 22-69-1.46
Christmas in Bernkastel 22-8-1.1
Christmas in Bremen 22-69-1.59; 22-69-1.5
Christmas in Bulgaria 26-69 1.3
Christmas in Church 14-8-1.74
Christmas in Cologne 22-69-1.61
Christmas in Copenhagen 14-8-1.62
Christmas in Dortland 22-8-1.6
Christmas in England 26-69-1.1
Christmas in Garmisch 22-69-1.62
Christmas in Greenland 14-8-1.78
Christmas in Holland 26-69-1.5
Christmas in Ireland 38-4-1.5
Christmas in Lubeck-Holstein 22-69-1.64
Christmas in Michelstadt 22-8-1.3
Christmas in Mexico 22-69-1.2
Christmas in Munich 22-6-1.6
Christmas in Norway 22-69-1.4
Christmas in Reginburg 22-69-1.58
Christmas in Rothenburg 22-69-1.60
Christmas in Rothenburg on Tauber . 22-8-1.2
Christmas in the Alps 22-69-1.20; 22-69-1.29; 22-69-1.43; 22-69-1.47
Christmas in the Forest 14-69-1.45; 22-69-1.41
Christmas in the Mountains 22-69-1.12; 22-69-1.17
Christmas in the Village 14-8-1.80
Christmas in Trafalgar Square 26-90-1.2
Christmas in Ulm 22-69-1.57
Christmas in Wendelstein 22-8-1.4
Christmas in Wurzburg 22-69-1.65
Christmas Lights 22-69-1.4
Christmas Market in Nurnberg 22-69-1.55
Christmas Meal of the Sparrows . . . 14-8-1.3
Christmas Message 72-72-1.1
Christmas Munich 22-69-1.56
Christmas Night 14-69-1.52
Christmas Night in a Village 22-77-1.3
Christmas Peace 22-69-1.36; 22-69-1.25
Christmas Prayer of the Sparrows . . 14-8-1.22
Christmas Rose and Cat 14-69-1.63

Christmas Roses and Christmas 14-8-1.4
Christmas Scene in Main Street 14-69-1.30
Christmas Sleigh Ride 22-6-1.7
Christmas Song 22-69-1.5
Christmas Star over the Sea and Sailing Ship 14-69-1.17
Christmas Story 14-38-1.3
Christmas Welcome 14-8-1.82
Church Bell in Tower 14-8-1.40
Church Bells Chiming in Christmas . 14-8-1.6; 14-8-2.2
Church in the Black Forest 22-6-1.8
Church Scene 54-61-1.1
Churchgoers on Christmas Day 14-8-1.32; 14-8-2.11
Cliff Gazing 38-4-2.3
Colette and Child 26-69-2.1
Collie 38-84-5.4
Cologne Cathedral 76-57-1.4
The Complete Gardener 14-40-2.7
Commemoration Cross in Honor of Danish Sailors Who Lost Their Lives in World War II 14-8-1.52
Composite 38-84-8.4
Consolation 22-73-2.1
La Contessa Isabella 22-69-6.1
The Continent Spanned 22-8-2.2
Cookout 54-61-3.2
Coquillage 18-46-1.8
Country Road in Autumn 22-6-4.3
Crossing the Delaware 84-34-1.4
The Crows Enjoying Christmas 14-8-1.5
Cyclamen 22-81-1.2

D

Dachshund 22-15-2.4; 38-84-5.5
Daisies for Mother 14-40-2.5
Dalecarlian Fiddler 76-69-1.5
Dancing Boy 38-48-3.2
Dancing Girl 38-48-3.1
Danish Farm on Christmas Night . . . 14-8-1.48
Danish Landscape 14-69-1.2; 14-69-1.4; 14-69-1.8; 14-69-1.16
Danish Mother 14-69-2.3
Danish Village Church 14-8-1.66; 14-69-1.34
Danish Watermill 14-69-1.69
Daughter and Doll 38-84-7.4
Dear Child 84-27-4.1
Deck the Halls 26-86-1.5
Declaration of Independence 84-34-1.1; 18-30-2.5
Declaration Signed 26-90-3.6
Decorating the Tree 42-85-3.2
Deer 38-84-3.1
Deer Family 22-23-1.5
Deers in the Woods 22-69-1.15
Delivering Christmas Letters 14-8-1.46
Deux Oiseaux 18-46-1.1
Devenish Island 34-8-1.5
Devotion for Mother 22-85-2.5
The Dillingen Madonna 22-69-1.38
Doberman 38-84-5.3
Doctor and the Doll 84-74-2.1
Dog and Puppies 14-8-3.1
Doe and Fawn 14-8-3.7; 22-77-3.2; 54-61-2.3
Doe and Fawns 22-15-2.1
A Doe and Her Fawn 22-8-3.6
Doe with Fawn 22-23-4.3
Domestic Employment 26-90-2.4
Doves 14-38-1.1
Downhill Daring 84-74-1.1

INDEX OF PLATE TITLES

A-11

Dreaming Lotus 26-69-4.2
Dreamrose 18-46-1.2
Duck and Ducklings 14-8-3.5
Duck Family 22-8-3.3; 22-77-3.5
Ducks 54-61-4.1
Dybbol Mill 14-8-1.53; 14-8-2.9

E

Eagle 18-46-1.12; 22-77-2.5
Easter Window 22-23-3.5
Ejby Kirken 22-13-1.4
Elderly Couple by Christmas Tree 14-69-1.5
Elephant 38-84-3.2
Elephant Mother and Baby 22-81-2.2
Elks 22-77-1.4
End of the Hunt 13-32-1.4
Eskimos Looking at Village Church
   in Greenland 14-8-1.34; 14-8-2.8
Expeditionary Ship in Pack-ice of
   Greenland 14-69-1.32

F

Falcon 38-84-4.2
Family Reunion 14-8-1.79
Fano Girl 14-69-1.48
Farm in Smaland 76-69-1.6
Father and Child 76-69-2.1
Father and Son 54-61-3.4
Feeding Time 22-77-1.7
Fetching the Christmas Tree 14-69-1.57
The Fir Tree and Hare 14-8-1.70
The Fir Tree 14-40-1.4
First Continental Congress 18-30-2.3
First It Was Sung by Angels to
   Shepherds in the Fields 14-8-1.17
The First Noel 84-84-1.3
First Thanksgiving 22-6-4.1
Fish Ballet 18-46-1.3
Fish Duet 18-46-1.11
Fisherman Sailing Home 76-69-1.2
Fisherman's Wharf (San Francisco) . . . 26-69-5.1
Fishing 54-61-3.1; 76-69-2.4
Fishing Boat off Kronborg Castle 14-69-1.28
Fishing Boats on the Way
   to the Harbor 14-69-1.23
Fishing Boat Returning Home for
   Christmas 14-8-1.24
Five Golden Rings 18-30-1.5
Flaming Heart 22-81-1.6
Fledglings 22-8-3.2
Flight into Egypt 18-15-2.1
Flight of Holy Family to Egypt 14-69-1.36
Flight of the Earls 34-8-1.3
Flowers for Mother 14-40-2.4; 22-42-2.2; 42-85-4.1; 76-57-2.1
Forest Chalet 'Serenity' 22-73-1.4
Four Colly Birds 18-30-1.4
Fox 22-42-2.4
Fox Outside Farm on Christmas Eve . . 14-8-1.35
Frederiksberg Gardens with Statue
   of Frederik VI 14-69-1.25
Frederiksborg Castle 14-69-1.46
Freiburg Cathedral 22-69-1.66

G

Gathering Easter Flowers 22-23-3.6
Gazelle Fantasie 18-46-1.4

German Shepherd 22-42-2.5; 38-84-5.1
Girl and Calf 54-61-2.7
Globe Trotter 22-27-1.3
Going to Church on Christmas 14-8-1.18
Goldfinch 84-50-1.2
Good Deeds 84-27-3.2
Good King Wenceslas 26-86-1.7
Good Night 14-40-2.3
The Good Shepherd 14-69-1.33; 14-69-1.40; 14-69-1.50
Goose Girl 22-27-1.4
Grandpa and Me 84-27-1.4
Grand Pals 84-27-1.6
The Great Belt Ferry 14-69-1.26
Greeland Mother 14-69-2.4
Green-winged Teal-Mallard 84-60-1.2
Grey Poodles 22-8-3.1
Group of Deer Under the Pines 22-69-1.21
Grundtvig Kirken 22-13-1.6
The Guardian Angel 22-85-1.4
Grundtvig Church, Copenhagen 14-69-1.22

H

Hanging the Wreath 84-23-1.5
Hans Christian Anderson House 14-40-1.1
Happiness over the Yule Tree 14-8-1.15
Happy Easter 22-47-3.1
Happy Expectation of Children 14-8-1.9
Hare in the Snow 14-69-1.64
Hark! The Herald Angels Sing 54-61-1.5; 84-66-2.3; 84-84-1.6
Harlequin 26-69-3.1
Harvest 22-6-4.2
Heavenly Angel 22-27-1.1
Heavenly Choir 38-48-1.3
Hear Ye, Hear Ye 22-27-1.2
Hedgehogs 22-23-4.2
The Hermitage Castle 14-69-1.27
Hibou 18-46-1.7
Hojsager Mill 14-69-1.56
The Holy Family 22-69-1.40
Holy Family and Angel 22-23-2.2
The Holy Light 22-69-1.44
Holy Night 22-42-1.4
Home for Christmas 14-8-1.72; 84-23-1.6
Home From the Fields 84-46-1.3
Horses Enjoying Christmas Meal
   in Stable 14-8-1.47; 14-8-2.13
The Houses of Parliament 26-90-1.6
Hummingbird 22-23-4.1
Hunting Scene 22-77-2.7

I

In Heaven the Angels Singing 26-86-1.2
In the Cradle 18-15-2.2
In the Desert 14-69-1.65
In the Park 14-69-1.12; 18-30-3.3; 22-42-3.2
Inauguration of George Washington . . 84-34-3.1
Incident at Concord Bridge 84-78-1.3
Interior of a Gothic Church 14-8-1.8
It Came Upon a Midnight Clear 84-84-1.4

J

Jayling 18-46-1.9
Jens Bang, New Passenger Boat
   Running Between Copenhagen and
   Aalborg 14-8-1.57

A-12

INDEX OF PLATE TITLES

Jesus and the Elders	54-61-1.9
Jesus on the Road to the Temple	54-61-1.8
Jingle Bells	84-84-1.2
The Joy of Christmas	22-47-1.5
Justinian	38-84-9.1

K

Kalundborg Church	14-8-1.61
Kalundborg Kirken	22-13-1.5
Kappl	22-6-1.2
King Balthazar	22-69-2.4
King Caspar	22-69-2.2
King Melchior	22-69-2.3
A Kiss for Lucy	42-85-2.4
Kiss of the Child	72-46-2.1
Knitting	38-4-3.5
Koala Bear and Cub	22-81-2.3; 22-23-4.5
The Korsor-Nyborg Ferry	14-8-1.39
Kristina and Child	26-69-2.3
Kronborg Castle at Elsinore	14-8-1.56; 14-8-2.10

L

Lamb	38-84-8.3
The Landing at North Island	18-15-1.2
The Landing of Columbus	22-8-2.3
Landsoldaten, 19th Century Danish Soldier	14-8-1.55
The Last Umiak	14-69-1.61
Lifeboat at Work	14-8-1.38
Lighting the Candles	14-8-1.44
Lillebelt Bridge Connecting Funen with Jutland	14-8-1.41
Linus and Snoopy	42-85-2.5
The Little Carolers	22-47-1.2
Little Drummer Boy	22-47-1.1
The Little Fisherman	22-85-2.2
Little Girl and her Brother	38-43-1.4
The Little Match Girl	14-8-1.13; 14-18-2.5; 14-40-1.2
The Little Mermaid at Wintertime	14-69-1.55
Little Mermaid of Copenhagen	14-40-1.3
Little Skaters	14-69-1.58
Lorgenfri Castle	14-8-1.50
Love Birds	22-42-3.1
Lynx Family	22-77-3.6

M

Madonna	38-48-1.2; 38-84-1.1
Madonna and Child	14-69-1.1; 22-69-2.1; 38-84-7.1; 38-84-7.2
Madonna by Murillo	18-32-2.4
Madonna by Rafael	18-32-2.1; 18-32-2.3
Madonnina by Feruzzi	18-32-2.2
The Magi	14-69-1.3
Maiden	38-43-3.4
Mallard	38-84-4.3
Man Fishing	22-77-2.2
The Manger in Bethlehem	22-69-1.11
Mare and Colt	22-15-2.2
Mare and Foal	14-8-3.4; 22-42-2.1; 54-61-2.1
Marianburg Castle	22-69-1.33
Marien Church in Danzig	22-69-1.31
Marilyn and Child	26-69-2.4
Marmor Kirken	22-13-1.3
Mary and Elizabeth	4-61-1.2
Mary with the Child Jesus	14-69-1.13

Me and My Pal	84-27-1.5
Meadowlark	84-50-1.4
Meal at Home	76-69-2.2
The Meeting at City Tavern	18-15-1.3
Mermaids	14-69-2.6
Message of Love	22-85-2.4
Message to the Shepherds	22-69-1.39
The Messages to Franklin	18-15-1.5
Midnight Mass	22-69-1.50
Midnight Mass at Kalundborg Church	22-77-1.2
The Midnight Ride of Paul Revere	84-34-1.2
Minnie Mouse and Friends	42-85-4.3
Mockingbird—Cardinal	84-60-1.3
Mom ?	42-85-2.2
Mother and Child	14-38-2.1; 14-69-1.24; 18-32-3.1; 22-47-2.1; 22-47-2.2; 22-47-2.3; 26-90-2.5; 72-46-2.4; 76-57-2.3; 76-57-2.4; 76-69-3.1; 84-23-2.1; 84-23-2.2; 84-23-2.3; 84-23-2.4; 72-46-2.6
Mother and Children	22-6-3.1; 22-6-3.2; 22-6-3.3; 22-6-3.4; 22-6-3.5; 72-46-2.3; 76-57-2.2; 22-69-5.1
Mother and Son	38-84-7.3
Mother Nursing	72-46-2.4
Mother Owl and Young	22-15-2.5
Motherly Love	38-48-3.3
Mother's Love	14-40-2.2
A Mother's Love	84-70-2.1
A Mother's World	14-38-2.3
Mountain Bluebird	84-50-1.3
Mountain Climber	22-77-2.3
Museum Plate	18-15-1.7
Musical Children	22-6-3.6
Myrtle Warbler and Cherry	26-78-1.2

N

The Nativity	4-61-1.6; 18-46-1.1; 22-85-1.3
New Moon over Snow-covered Trees	14-8-1.2
Niklas Church	22-15-1.2
Nils in Lapland	76-69-1.4
Nils in Vastmanland	76-69-1.8
Nils with His Geese	76-69-1.3
No Room at the Inn	4-61-1.4
Nodebo Church at Christmastime	14-69-1.41
Notre Dame Cathedral	76-57-1.1
Nurnberg Angel	22-69-1.27

O

O Holy Night	84-84-1.5
Old Copenhagen Canals at Wintertime, with Thorvaldsen Museum in Background	14-8-1.58
The Old Grist Mill	84-78-2.2
The Old Farmyard	14-69-1.62
Old-Fashioned Picnic	76-69-3.3
Old Mill	22-6-4.4; 22-73-1.3
The Old North Church	38-84-11.2
The Old Organist	14-8-1.16; 14-8-2.4
The Old Water Mill	14-8-1.51; 14-8-1.81
The Old West	84-27-2.1
Ole Lock-Eye, The Sandman	14-8-1.45
Once Upon a Summertime	22-69-3.1

INDEX OF PLATE TITLES

Orchid 22-81-1.1
Oriental Mother 14-69-2.2
Our Lady's Cathedral, Copenhagen . . . 14-69-1.42
Outside the Lighted Window 14-8-1.25
Owl 38-84-4.1
Owl Family 22-77-3.4

P

Papillon 18-30-1.1; 18-46-1.5; 26-86-1.1
A Partridge in a Pear Tree 18-30-1.1; 26-86-1.1; 84-66-2.1; 84-84-1.1
Path of the Magi 22-69-1.22
Paul Revere's Ride 26-90-3.2
Peace on Earth 22-47-1.3; 22-69-1.9
A Peaceful Motif 14-69-1.38
Peacock 18-46-1.6
Pelican 38-84-9.2
Persian 38-84-10.1
Pheasants in the Snow at Christmas . . 14-8-1.76
Picadilly Circus, London 26-90-1.3
Pierrot 26-69-3.2
Pigeons in the Castle Court 14-8-1.27
Pine Siskin 84-66-1.1
Pink Carnation 38-48-2.1
Pinky and Baby 18-32-3.2
Pipers at Alberobello 38-4-1.2
Playing Hooky 22-85-2.1
Pontius on the Floor 76-69-3.5
Poodle 38-84-5.2
A President's Wife 84-46-1.4
Promise of the Savior 54-61-1.6
Promises to Keep 84-27-4.2
Puma 38-84-3.3
Puppy Love 84-74-2.2
Pussy Willows 22-23-3.4

Q

Queen's Palace 14-69-1.68

R

Rabbit Family 22-77-3.3
Rabbits 22-23-1.1; 22-23-3.3; 22-27-4.1; 38-84-8.1; 84-50-3.3
Raccoons 84-50-3.1
Red Cardinal 84-66-1.4
Red Fox 84-50-3.2
Red Roses 38-48-2.2
Red-shouldered Hawk 84-66-1.2
Redstarts and Beech 26-78-1.1
Regatta 22-77-2.6
The Ribe Cathedral 14-8-1.49; 22-13-1.2
Ride into Christmas 22-27-1.5
Ride of Paul Revere 18-30-2.4; 84-78-1.2
Riding to Hunt 84-23-3.3
Rigoletto 38-72-1.1
Road to Bethlehem 4-61-1.3; 54-61-1.3
The Road — Winter 84-78-2.1
Robin 22-27-2.1
Rocking the Cradle 22-6-3.8
Rosenborg Castle, Copenhagen 14-69-1.49
Roses 22-81-2.1
Roskilde Cathedral 14-69-1.29; 22-13-1.1
Rothenberg Scene 22-15-1.5
Round Church in Osterlars on Bornholm 14-69-1.31

A-13

Royal Boat in Greenland Waters 14-8-1.59
Royal Castle of Amalienborg, Copenhagen 14-8-1.20; 14-8-2.12
Royal Copenhagen Bicentennial 14-69-3.1
Royal Guard Outside Amalienborg Castle in Copenhagen 14-8-1.42; 14-8-2.7
Royal Hunting Castle, the Ermitage . . 14-8-1.29
The Royal Oak 14-69-1.60
Royal Street (New Orleans) 26-69-5.2
Rufous Hummingbird 84-50-1.5

S

Sacred Journey 22-85-2.5
Sailing 38-4-2.4
Sailing with the Tide 26-69-6.1
St. Christopher with the Christ Child 22-69-1.10
St. Jokob in Groden 38-4-1.1
St. Paul's Cathedral 26-90-1.4
St. Petri Church of Copenhagen 14-8-1.14
Santa Claus 14-8-1.64
Sarah en Tournure 18-15-3.2
Sayuri and Child 26-69-2.2
Scarlet en Crinoline 18-15-3.1
Schneekoppe Mountain 22-69-1.30
Schwanstein Church 22-15-1.3
Scotty Gets His Tree 84-70-1.1
Sct. Knuds Kirken 22-13-1.8
The Secret Contract 18-15-1.1
Serenade to Lovers 22-42-3.5
Seven Swans A' Swimming 18-30-1.7
The Sewing Lesson 26-90-2.2
Sharing the Joy of Christmas 14-8-1.73
Sheep 22-23-3.1
Sheep and Shepherds 14-69-1.11
Sheep in the Field 54-61-4.5
Shelling Peas 76-69-3.2
Shepherd in the Field on Christmas Night 14-69-1.9
Shepherd Scene 22-15-1.1
Shepherds 38-84-2.2; 54-61-1.7
Shepherds in the Field 4-61-1.5
Ship's Boy at the Tiller on Christmas Night 14-69-1.20
Siamese 38-84-10.2
The Siege at Yorktown 18-15-1.6
Signing of the Declaration of Independence 84-78-1.4
Silent Night 22-42-1.2; 22-69-1.54
Silver Pennies 18-46-1.10
Six Geese A' Laying 18-30-1.6
Skating 54-61-3.5
Skating Couple 14-8-1.33
Skating on the Brandywine 84-23-3.4
Skiing 54-61-3.6
Sledding 54-61-3.3
Sleighing to Church on Christmas 14-8-1.12
Sleigh-ride 42-85-3.1
Snoopy & Woodstock on Parade 42-85-2.3
Snoopy Guides the Sleigh 42-85-1.1
Snow Scene 22-73-1.2
Snow White & the Seven Dwarfs . . . 42-85-4.2
Snowman 22-6-1.9
Snowy Village 22-23-1.2
Solitary Christmas 22-69-1.52
Son and Daughter 38-84-7.5
Sparrows 22-23-1.4
Sparrows in Tree at Church of the Holy Spirit, Copenhagen 14-69-1.7

INDEX OF PLATE TITLES

Spire of Frederik's Church, Copenhagen	14-69-1.6
The Spinner	26-90-2.6
Spirit of Christmas	72-72-1.5
Sportive Love	26-90-2.1
Spring	18-12-1.3; 42-72-2.1
Spring Harmony	26-69-4.1
Spring Outing	22-6-3.7
Spring-time	22-47-3.2
Squirrels	22-8-3.4; 22-81-2.4
The Stag	14-69-1.53
Stand at Concord Bridge	84-34-1.3
Star of Bethlehem	14-8-1.28; 22-69-1.42
Stardust	22-69-1.3
Start of the Hunt	18-32-1.2
Station on the Way	22-69-1.18
Stiftskirche	22-6-1.1
Stilt Sandpiper	84-66-1.3
Stormy Weather	22-27-3.1
Strassburg Cathedral	22-69-1.32
Street Scene from Christianshavn, Copenhagen	14-69-1.18
Summer	18-12-1.1
Sunbonnet Babies	22-73-3.1
Sunflowers	22-81-1.5
Sunshine over Greenland	14-69-1.51
Surprise for Mother	14-40-2.6
Surrender at Yorktown	84-34-1.6
Swan and Brood	22-77-3.1
Swan and Cygnets	22-42-2.6
Swan Family	14-8-3.8; 22-23-4.4; 22-81-2.5
Sweet Dreams	14-38-2.2
Sweethearts	42-72-1.1

T

Tabby	38-84-5.5
Temple Rue de la Victoire, Paris	76-57-1.5
Tender Moment	22-42-3.4
Thanksgiving on the Farm	22-6-4.6
Three Apostles	38-84-6.1; 38-84-6.2; 38-84-6.3; 38-84-6.4
Three French Hens	18-30-1.3
Three Kings	38-84-2.1; 54-61-1.2
Three Singing Angels	14-69-1.15
The Three Wise Men	18-46-1.2; 22-23-2.1; 22-69-1.16; 22-69-1.2; 72-74-1.2
The Three Wise Men from the East	14-8-1.7; 14-8-2.6
Thru the Night to Light	22-69-1.24
Tiger	38-84-3.4
Tiger and Cub	22-15-2.3
Tilling the Fields	76-69-2.3
Tiny Tim	84-27-3.1; 84-34-2.1
To Market	18-30-3.4
Tom Thumb	22-15-2.5
Tower Bridge	26-90-1.7
The Tower of London	26-90-1.5
Tower of Our Savior's Church, Copenhagen	14-69-1.10
Toys for Sale	22-6-1.5
Train Homeward Bound for Christmas	14-69-1.66
Training Ship Danmark	14-69-1.54
Tribute to W. B. Yeats	34-8-1.4
Trimming the Tree	84-23-1.4
The Truth About Santa	84-46-1.2
Tulips	22-81-1.4
Two Turtle Doves	18-30-1.2
Typical Danish Winter Scene	14-69-1.37

U

The Ugly Duckling	14-40-1.6
Under the Mistletoe	84-23-1.2
The Unicorn in Captivity	18-32-1.1
The Unicorn is Brought to the Castle	18-32-1.6
The Unicorn Surrounded	18-32-1.5
United States Bicentennial	14-69-3.2
U.S. Frigate Constitution	22-77-2.1

V

Vadstena	76-69-1.7
Victorian Boy and Girl	26-69-7.1
View of Christianshavn Canal	14-69-1.19
View of Copenhagen from Frederiksberg Hill	14-8-1.10
Vicar's Family on Way to Church	14-69-1.21
Victory at Yorktown	26-90-3.5
Village at Christmas	22-77-1.6
Village Scene	22-15-1.4

W

Waiting for Santa Claus	22-42-1.1
Walking to Church	22-69-1.6
The Wash	18-30-3.2
Washington Crossing the Delaware	22-8-2.5; 84-78-1.5
Watchman, Sculpture of Town Hall, Copenhagen	14-8-1.54
We Saw Three Ships A-Sailing	26-86-1.3
We Three Kings of Orient Are	22-86-1.4; 84-66-2.2
We Wish You Happiness, Mother	22-47-2.4
Welcome Home	22-42-1.3
Westminster Abbey	76-57-1.2
White-tailed Deer	84-60-1.6
Wild Deer in Forest	22-6-4.5
Wild Turkey—Ring-Necked Pheasant	84-60-1.4
Windsor Castle	26-90-1.1
Winter	18-12-1.4
Winter Birds	22-23-1.6
Winter Fox	84-23-3.2
Winter Harmony	14-8-1.67
Winter Idyll	22-69-1.34
Winter Night	14-8-1.68
Winter Peace	22-69-1.1
Winter Scene	14-38-1.4
Winter Twilight	14-69-1.67
With Love to You at Easter	22-47-3.3
Wood Scape	22-69-1.35
Wood Thrush	84-50-1.1
Woodcock and Young	22-77-3.7
Woodcock—Ruffed Grouse	84-60-1.1
Woodstock, Santa Claus	42-85-1.4
Woodstock's Christmas	42-85-1.5
Wurzburg Castle	22-6-2.6

Y

Yellow Breasted Chat	84-66-1.6
Yellow Dahlia	38-48-2.3
Young America, 1776	84-50-2.2
Young Americans	22-73-2.2
Young Americans II	22-73-2.3
Young Americans III	22-73-2.4
Young Love	84-27-1.2
Young Man and Girl	38-4-1.4
Yule Tree in Town Hall Square of Copenhagen	14-8-1.36
Zealand Village Church	14-69-1.39

INDEX OF PLATE ARTISTS

A
Aarestrup 14-8-1.15
Audubon, John 84-66-1.1; 84-66-1.2; 84-66-1.3;
84-66-1.4; 84-66-1.5; 84-66-1.6;
84-66-2.1; 84-66-2.2; 84-66-2.3;
84-66-2.4; 84-66-2.5; 84-66-2.6;
84-66-1.7

B
Baaring, Maggi 14-40-2.1
Bauer, Kurt 22-42-1.2; 22-42-1.3; 22-42-1.5
Beilefeld, Kurt C. 22-6-4.1; 22-6-4.2; 22-6-4.3;
22-6-4.4; 22-6-4.5; 22-6-4.6
Bocher, R. 14-69-1.9; 14-69-1.19; 14-69-1.29;
14-69-1.38; 14-69-1.44
Bochmann, Gerhard . . 22-27-4.1; 22-27-4.2
Boehm, Edward 84-50-1.1; 84-50-1.2; 84-50-1.3;
84-50-1.4; 84-50-1.5; 84-50-2.1;
84-50-2.2; 84-50-3.1; 84-50-3.2;
84-50-3.3
Boesen, A. 14-69-1.6; 14-69-1.7
Bonfils, Kjeld 14-8-1.59; 14-8-1.61; 14-8-1.62;
14-8-1.63; 14-8-1.64; 14-8-1.65;
14-8-1.66; 14-8-1.67; 14-8-1.68
Bratlie, Gunnar 54-61-1.1; 54-61-1.2; 54-61-1.3;
54-61-1.4; 54-61-1.5; 54-61-1.6;
54-61-1.7; 54-61-1.8; 54-61-1.9;
54-61-2.1; 54-61-2.2; 54-61-2.3;
54-61-2.4; 54-61-2.5; 54-61-2.6;
54-61-2.7; 54-61-3.1; 54-61-3.2;
54-61-3.3; 54-61-3.4; 54-61-3.5;
54-61-3.6; 54-61-4.1; 54-61-4.2;
54-61-4.3; 54-61-4.4; 54-61-4.5

C
Carlsen, Marion 18-32-3.1; 18-32-3.2
Castrejon, Chavela 26-69-1.2
Corbett, Bertha L. 22-73-3.1
Crewe, Emma 26-90-2.2
Currier & Ives 84-78-1.1; 84-78-1.2; 84-78-1.3;
84-78-1.4; 84-78-2.1; 84-78-2.2

D
DeMille, Leslie 22-69-5.1
Dier, Amadeus 22-69-1.34
Dietz, Julius 22-69-1.4
Disney, Walt 42-85-3.1; 42-85-3.2; 42-85-3.3;
42-85-4.1; 42-85-4.2; 42-85-4.3;
42-85-3.4
Drexler, Helmut 22-69-1.66; 22-69-1.67

E
Eriksen, Edward 14-40-1.3
Ersgaard 14-8-1.16; 14-8-2.4

F
Falchi, Aldo 38-43-1.3; 38-43-3.3; 38-43-3.4;
38-43-1.4
Fennel, Tom Jr. 4-61-1.1
Feruzzi 18-32-2.2
Fink, Heinrich 22-69-1.19; 22-69-1.20; 22-69-1.22;
22-69-1.25; 22-69-1.26; 22-69-1.27;
22-69-1.28; 22-69-1.29; 22-69-1.30
Flugenring, H. 14-8-1.36; 14-8-1.38; 14-8-1.39
Franka, Ozz 22-73-2.1
Friis, Achton 14-8-1.23; 14-8-1.24; 14-8-1.25;
14-8-1.26; 14-8-1.27; 14-8-1.28;
14-8-1.29; 14-8-1.30; 14-8-1.31;
14-8-1.32; 14-8-1.33; 14-8-1.34;
14-8-1.35; 14-8-1.37; 14-8-2.8;
14-8-2.11

G
Gahries, I. 22-23-1.6; 22-23-3.6; 22-23-4.5
Ganeau, Francois 18-15-3.1; 18-15-3.2
Garde, Fanny 14-8-1.4
Groote, Anne V. 22-69-1.42
Grossberg, Eva 22-23-2.1; 22-23-2.2; 22-23-2.3
Guldrandson, Jul. V. . . . 22-69-1.1; 22-69-1.6; 22-69-1.7

H
Hackwood, William . . . 26-90-2.6
Hagen, Louis 22-69-1.38
Hallin, F. A. 14-8-1.1; 14-8-1.2; 14-8-1.3;
14-8-2.1
Hansen, Einar 14-8-1.18
Hansen, Hans H. 14-69-1.42; 14-69-1.50; 14-69-1.51;
14-69-1.52; 14-69-1.53
Harper, Tom 26-90-1.1; 26-90-1.2; 26-90-1.3;
26-90-1.4; 26-90-1.5; 26-90-1.6;
26-90-1.7
Hein, Willi 22-69-1.35; 22-69-1.37; 22-69-1.41;
22-69-1.43; 22-69-1.44; 22-69-1.45;
22-69-1.46; 22-69-1.47; 22-69-1.48;
22-69-1.49; 22-69-1.50; 22-69-1.51;
22-69-1.52; 22-69-1.53; 22-69-1.54
Hetreau, Remy 18-30-1.1; 18-30-1.2; 18-30-1.3;
18-30-1.4; 18-30-1.5; 18-30-1.6;
18-30-2.1; 18-30-2.2; 18-30-2.3;
18-30-2.4; 18-30-3.1; 18-30-3.2;
18-30-3.3; 18-30-3.4; 18-30-2.5
Hibel, Edna 26-69-2.1; 26-69-2.2; 26-69-2.3;
22-69-6.1
Hofer, Ernst 22-69-1.14
Hoffman, Richard 22-69-1.39
Hummel, Berta 22-85-1.1; 22-85-1.2; 22-85-1.3;
22-85-1.4; 22-85-1.5; 22-85-1.6;
22-85-2.1; 22-85-2.2; 22-85-2.3;
22-85-2.4; 22-85-2.5; 22-27-3.1;
22-27-1.1; 22-27-1.2; 22-27-1.3;
22-27-1.4; 22-27-1.5
Hyldahl, Magrethe 14-8-1.9; 14-8-1.52; 14-8-1.53;
14-8-1.54; 14-8-1.55; 14-8-1.56;
14-8-1.57; 14-8-2.9; 14-8-2.10

J
Jansen, Leo 22-73-2.2; 22-73-2.3; 22-73-2.4
Jensen, Dahl 14-8-1.5; 14-8-1.6; 14-8-1.8;

INDEX OF PLATE ARTISTS

Jensen, Oluf	14-8-1.11; 14-8-1.12; 14-8-1.21; 14-8-2.2; 14-8-2.3
	14-69-1.4; 14-69-1.10; 14-69-1.11; 14-69-1.12; 14-69-1.14; 14-69-1.16; 14-69-1.18; 14-69-1.22; 14-69-1.25; 14-69-1.27
Jorgensen, J. Bloch	14-8-1.14

K

Karl, Prof.	22-69-1.40
Karner, Theo	22-69-1.15; 22-69-1.21
Kingman, Doug	26-69-5.1; 26-69-5.2
Kjolner, Th.	14-69-1.34; 14-69-1.41; 14-69-1.45
Koch, Otto	22-69-1.23
Krog, A.	14-69-1.8
Kuspert, Georg	22-69-1.55; 22-69-1.56; 22-69-1.57; 22-69-1.58; 22-69-1.59; 22-69-1.60; 22-69-1.61; 22-69-1.62; 22-69-1.63; 22-69-1.64; 22-69-1.65

L

Lalique, Marie Claude	18-46-1.1; 18-46-1.2; 18-46-1.3; 18-46-1.4; 18-46-1.5; 18-46-1.6; 18-46-1.7; 18-46-1.8; 18-46-1.9; 18-46-1.10; 18-46-1.11; 18-46-1.12
Lange, Kai	14-69-1.33; 14-69-1.40; 14-69-1.45; 14-69-1.47; 14-69-1.48; 14-69-1.49; 14-69-1.54; 14-69-1.56; 14-69-1.57; 14-69-1.58; 14-69-1.59; 14-69-1.60; 14-69-1.61; 14-69-1.62; 14-69-1.63; 14-69-1.64; 14-69-1.65; 14-69-1.66; 14-69-1.67; 14-69-1.68; 14-69-1.69
Larsen, Ove	14-8-1.41; 14-8-1.42; 14-8-1.43; 14-8-1.46; 14-8-1.47; 14-8-1.48; 14-8-1.49; 14-8-1.50; 14-8-1.51; 14-8-2.7; 14-8-2.13
Larsen, Th.	14-8-1.19; 14-8-1.20; 14-8-2.12
Larsson, Carl	76-69-2.1; 76-69-2.2; 76-69-2.3; 76-69-2.4; 76-69-3.1; 76-69-3.2; 76-69-3.3; 76-69-3.4; 76-69-3.5
Lihs, Helmut	22-47-1.1; 22-47-1.2; 22-47-1.3; 22-47-1.4; 22-47-2.1; 22-47-2.2; 22-47-2.3; 22-47-2.4; 22-47-3.1; 22-47-3.2; 22-47-3.3; 22-47-1.5
Lladro, Juan	72-46-1.1; 72-46-1.2; 72-46-1.3; 72-46-1.4; 72-46-2.1; 72-46-2.2; 72-46-2.3; 72-46-2.4; 72-46-2.5; 72-46-2.5
Lockhart, James	84-60-1.1; 84-60-1.2; 84-60-1.3; 84-60-1.4; 84-60-1.5; 84-60-1.6

M

Maratta, Cark	22-42-1.7
Merli, Bruno	38-43-1.1; 38-43-1.2; 38-43-3.1; 38-43-3.2
Moere	22-69-1.8
Moltke, H.	14-8-1.17
Mueller, Hans	22-6-1.1; 22-6-1.2; 22-6-1.3; 22-6-1.4; 22-6-1.6; 22-6-1.7; 22-6-1.8; 22-6-1.9; 22-6-2.1; 22-6-2.2; 22-6-2.3; 22-6-2.4; 22-6-2.5; 22-6-2.6; 22-6-2.7; 22-6-2.6; 22-6-1.10
Mundel, Alfred	22-69-1.36
Murillo	18-32-2.4
Mutze, Walter	22-69-1.31; 22-69-1.32; 22-69-1.33

N

Nast, Thomas	84-34-2.2
Negro, Hans	22-81-1.1; 22-81-1.2; 22-81-1.3; 22-81-1.4; 22-81-1.5; 22-81-1.6; 22-81-2.1; 22-81-2.2; 22-81-2.3; 22-81-2.4; 22-81-2.5
Neiman, Leroy	26-69-3.1; 26-69-3.2
Neubauer, Josef	22-47-1.1; 22-47-1.2; 22-47-1.3; 22-47-1.4; 22-47-3.1; 22-47-3.2; 22-47-3.3; 22-47-2.1; 22-47-2.2; 22-47-2.3; 22-47-2.4
Nicolai, F.	22-69-1.13
Nielsen, Herne	14-69-1.31
Nielsen, Sv. Nic.	14-69-1.32
Northcott, Joann	22-42-1.6
Nylund, Gunnar	76-69-1.1; 76-69-1.2; 76-69-1.3; 76-69-1.4; 76-69-1.5; 76-69-1.6; 76-69-1.7; 76-69-1.8

O

Oigaard, Nulle	14-40-2.2
Oliveiro, Manuel de	84-34-1.1; 84-34-1.2; 84-34-1.3; 84-34-1.4; 84-34-1.5; 84-34-1.6
Olsen, Benjamin	14-69-1.17; 14-69-1.20; 14-69-1.23; 14-69-1.26; 14-69-1.28
Olsen, Cathinka	14-8-1.10
Olsen, Viggo	14-69-1.37; 14-69-1.43
Otto, Svend	14-40-1.4; 14-40-1.5; 14-40-1.6

P

Pfeiffer	22-69-1.9
Plockross, E.	14-8-1.13; 14-8-2.5
Poillerat, Gilbert	18-12-1.1; 18-12-1.2; 18-12-1.3; 18-12-1.4; 18-12-2.1
Polusynski, Jack	22-77-1.1; 22-77-1.2; 22-77-1.3; 22-77-1.4; 22-77-1.5; 22-77-1.6; 22-77-1.7; 22-77-2.1; 22-77-2.2; 22-77-2.3; 22-77-2.4; 22-77-2.5; 22-77-2.6; 22-77-3.1; 22-77-3.2; 22-77-3.3; 22-77-3.4; 22-77-3.5; 22-77-3.6; 22-77-3.7; 22-77-2.7; 22-77-1.8
Popelier, Roch	18-69-1.1; 18-69-1.2
Pramvig, Borge	14-8-1.58; 14-8-1.60

R

Ranck, Gloria	42-72-2.1
Rafael	18-32-2.1; 18-32-2.3
Reith, Paul	22-69-1.3
Remington, Fredrick	84-27-2.1
Restieau, Andre	18-15-1.1; 18-15-1.2; 18-15-1.3; 18-15-1.4; 18-15-1.5; 18-15-1.6; 18-15-1.7; 18-15-2.1; 18-15-2.2
Richter, Ludwig	22-6-1.5; 22-6-3.1; 22-6-3.2; 22-6-3.3; 22-6-3.4; 22-6-3.5; 22-6-3.6; 22-6-3.7; 22-6-3.8
Rockwell, Norman	42-72-1.1; 84-23-1.1; 84-23-1.2; 84-23-1.2; 84-23-1.3; 84-23-1.4; 84-23-1.5; 84-23-1.6; 84-27-1.1; 84-27-1.2; 84-27-1.3; 84-27-1.4; 84-27-1.5; 84-27-3.1; 84-27-3.2; 84-46-1.1; 84-46-1.2; 84-46-1.3; 84-70-1.1; 84-70-1.2; 84-70-2.1; 84-74-1.1; 84-74-2.1; 84-27-1.6; 84-74-2.2
Rode, G.	14-69-1.13; 14-69-1.21; 14-69-1.24
Rotger, Georg	22-73-1.4
Ruggeri, Gino	38-72-1.1

INDEX OF PLATE ARTISTS　　　　　　　　　　　　A-17

S

Sabra, S. 14-8-1.7; 14-8-2.6
Sales, Harry 26-69-1.1
Saustuart, Gerhard 14-40-1.1
Schertel, Dr. W 22-69-1.10; 22-69-1.11
Schiffner, Hans 22-69-1.24
Schmutz-Baudess, Theo. 22-69-1.17; 22-69-1.18
Schoen, Walter 22-23-1.1; 22-23-1.2; 22-23-1.3; 22-23-1.4; 22-23-1.5
Schoener, Toni 22-42-1.1; 22-42-1.4; 22-42-2.1; 22-42-2.2; 22-42-2.3; 22-42-2.4; 22-42-2.5; 22-42-2.6; 22-42-3.1; 22-42-3.2; 22-42-3.3; 22-42-3.4; 22-42-3.5
Schultz, Charles 42-85-1.1; 42-85-1.2; 42-85-1.3; 42-85-1.4; 42-85-1.5; 42-85-2.1; 42-85-2.2; 42-85-2.3; 42-85-2.4; 42-85-2.5
Selbing, John 76-57-1.1; 76-57-1.2; 76-57-1.3; 76-57-1.4; 76-57-1.5; 76-57-1.6; 76-57-1.7; 76-57-2.1; 76-57-2.2; 76-57-2.3; 76-57-2.4; 76-57-2.5; 76-57-2.6
Selschou-Olsen 14-69-1.15
Sparks, Gerry 4-61-1.2; 4-61-1.3; 4-61-1.4; 4-61-1.5; 4-61-1.6
Spencer, Irene 84-23-2.1; 84-23-2.2; 84-23-2.3; 84-23-2.4; 84-27-4.1; 84-27-4.2
Stage, Mads 14-40-1.2; 14-40-2.3; 14-40-2.4; 14-40-2.5; 14-40-2.6; 14-40-2.7
Stobart, John 26-69-6.1
Sanberg, Carl 84-34-2.1
Svensson, Kamma 14-69-2.1; 14-69-2.2

T

Tauschek 22-69-1.16
Templetown, Lady Eliz. . 26-90-2.1; 26-90-2.3; 26-90-2.4; 26-90-2.5
Thelander, Henry 14-8-1.69; 14-8-1.70; 14-8-1.71; 14-8-1.72; 14-8-1.73; 14-8-1.74; 14-8-1.75; 14-8-1.76; 14-8-1.77; 14-8-1.78; 14-8-1.79; 14-8-1.80; 14-8-1.81; 14-8-1.82; 14-8-3.1; 14-8-3.2; 14-8-3.3; 14-8-3.4; 14-8-3.5; 14-8-3.6; 14-8-3.7; 14-8-3.8
Thomsen, Chr. 14-69-1.1; 14-69-1.3; 14-69-1.5
Thorsson, Nils 14-69-1.30; 14-69-1.35; 14-69-1.36; 14-69-1.39
Tiziano, Vincente 38-84-1.1; 38-84-2.1; 38-84-2.2; 38-84-2.3; 38-84-2.4; 38-84-3.1; 38-84-3.2; 38-84-3.3; 38-84-3.4; 38-84-4.1; 38-84-4.2; 38-84-4.2; 38-84-4.3; 38-84-5.1; 38-84-5.2; 38-84-5.3; 38-84-5.4; 38-84-6.1; 38-84-6.2; 38-84-6.3; 38-84-7.1; 38-84-7.2; 38-84-7.3; 38-84-7.4; 38-84-7.5; 38-84-8.1; 38-84-8.2; 38-84-8.3; 38-84-8.4; 38-84-9.1; 38-84-9.2; 38-84-10.1; 38-84-10.2; 38-84-11.1; 38-84-11.2; 38-84-10.3; 38-84-5.5
Tjerne, Immanuel 14-8-1.40; 14-8-1.44; 14-8-1.45
Toby, Alton 26-69-1.4; 26-69-1.5
Trester, Irene 22-69-3.1

U

Ungermann, Arne 14-69-2.3; 14-69-2.4; 14-69-2.5; 14-69-2.6
Ussing, St. 14-69-1.2

V

Varnazza, Sandro 38-43-2.1; 38-43-2.2; 38-43-2.3; 38-43-2.4
Vestergaard, Sven 14-69-3.1; 14-69-3.2
Vidal, Hahn 26-69-4.1; 26-69-4.2
Vinci, Leonardo da 38-64-6.1; 38-64-6.2; 38-64-6.3; 38-64-6.4; 38-64-6.5
Vogoler, Heinrich 22-69-1.2

W

Waldheimer, Hans 22-15-1.1; 22-15-1.2; 22-15-1.3; 22-15-1.4; 22-15-1.5; 22-15-2.1; 22-15-2.2; 22-15-2.3; 22-15-2.4; 22-15-1.6; 22-15-1.5
West Gillian 26-86-1.1; 26-86-1.2; 26-86-1.3; 26-86-1.4; 26-86-1.5; 26-86-1.6; 26-86-1.7
Wiertz, Jupp 22-69-1.12
Wiinblad, Bjorn 22-69-2.1; 22-69-2.2; 22-69-2.3; 22-69-2.4; 22-69-2.5; 22-69-2.6; 22-69-4.1
Wyeth, James 84-23-3.1; 84-23-3.2; 84-23-3.3; 84-23-3.4; 84-23-3.5

Y

Yordanov, Dimitri 26-69-1.3

Z

Zumbusch, Profil V. . . . 22-69-1.5

The editors acknowledge with gratitude the invaluable supplementary information supplied by:

Armstrong's
  Dave Armstrong
Bing & Grondahl Copenhagen Porcelain, Inc.
  Joan Doyle
  Jorgen Sonnung
Commemorative Imports
  Don Hershleb
Creative World, Ltd.
  Lee Benson
D'Arceau Limoges
  Gerard Boyer
Ebeling & Reuss Co.
  George W. Ebeling
Fisher, Bruce & Co.
  Robert D. Murray
  Robert H. Westermann
Gorham Silver Co.
  Edward Purcell
Haviland & Co., Inc.
  George Armstrong
  Laverne Zohimsky
Helmut H. Lins Imports
  Helmut H. Lihs
Hollywood Art Galleries
  Bill Freudenberg
  Chip Freudenberg
Hummelwerk
  James P. Kelly
  James Lerner
International Silver Co.
  Cindy Haskins
Jacques Jugeat, Inc.
  Lloyd Glasgow
Georg Jensen
  Raymond Zrike
Svend Jensen
  Per Jensen
  Erik Larsen
Jon Nielsen's Import Co.
  Jon Nielsen
Joy's Limited
  Jim Petrozzini
Kaiser Porcelain Co.
  Hubert E. W. Kaiser
K & L Publications
  Louise Witt

Lake Shore Prints, Inc.
  Donald H. Detlefsen
Pickard China Co.
  Henry Pickard
Porcelana Granada
  Trudy Fennell
Rasmussen Import Co.
  R. D. Rasmussen
Reco International Corp.
  Dorothy George
  Heio Reich
Reed & Barton
  Charles French
  Stafford P. Osborn
Rosenthal U.S.A. Limited
  Susan Strong
  Klaus Vogt
Royal Copenhagen Porcelain Corp.
  Ivar Ipsen
Royal Doulton Co.
  E. T. Catlett
  Nancy Clark
Royal Worcester Porcelain Co., Inc.
  Bessie Jimenez
Schmid Brothers
  Siegfried Claussner
  Paul Schmid, Sr.
Spode, Inc.
  Chris C. Church
The Franklin Mint
  Jo Solidoro
Trein's
  Gordon Brantley
Vernonware
  Doug Bothwell
  Joe Powers
Viking Import House
  Pat Owen
Wara Intercontinental Co.
  Walter A. Rautenberg
Josiah Wedgwood & Sons, Inc.
  Claudia Coleman
  Harvey Dondero
Weil Ceramic & Glass, Inc.
  Charles Morgan

YOUR FREE SUBSCRIPTION FORM TO THE "BRADEX"

Your purchase of *The Bradford Book of Collector's Plates* entitles you to a free one-year subscription to the "Bradex"—The Bradford Exchange Current Quotations.

The "Bradex" is the standard comprehensive report of current market prices as quoted on the floor of the world's largest trading center for all 859 collector' plates listed in this *Bradford Book*. These are the prices at which you can trade and are a reflection of market movement.

To obtain your free subscription, simply write your name and address on the form below, cut it out, and fold to form a postage-free envelope.

The Bradford Exchange
Lockbox 48-204
Chicago, Illinois
60648

Retain for your records:

Date sent: _____

(Cut on dotted line, fold A to B, fold flap and staple or seal with tape)

A

BRADFORD EXCHANGE FORM CJ-7
FREE ONE-YEAR SUBSCRIPTION TO THE "BRADEX"

Date: _____

Dear Sirs:

Please enter my one-year subscription to the "Bradex"—the standard comprehensive report of current market prices for all plates traded on the Exchange. I understand this report is issued bi-monthly, that I will receive six issues beginning with the most recent, and that there will be no charge or obligation for this service.

Fold

Name _____

Address _____

City _____

State _____ Zip _____

Fold

B

To receive your FREE "Bradex" subscription,
Cut out, fold, seal, and mail. No postage necessary.

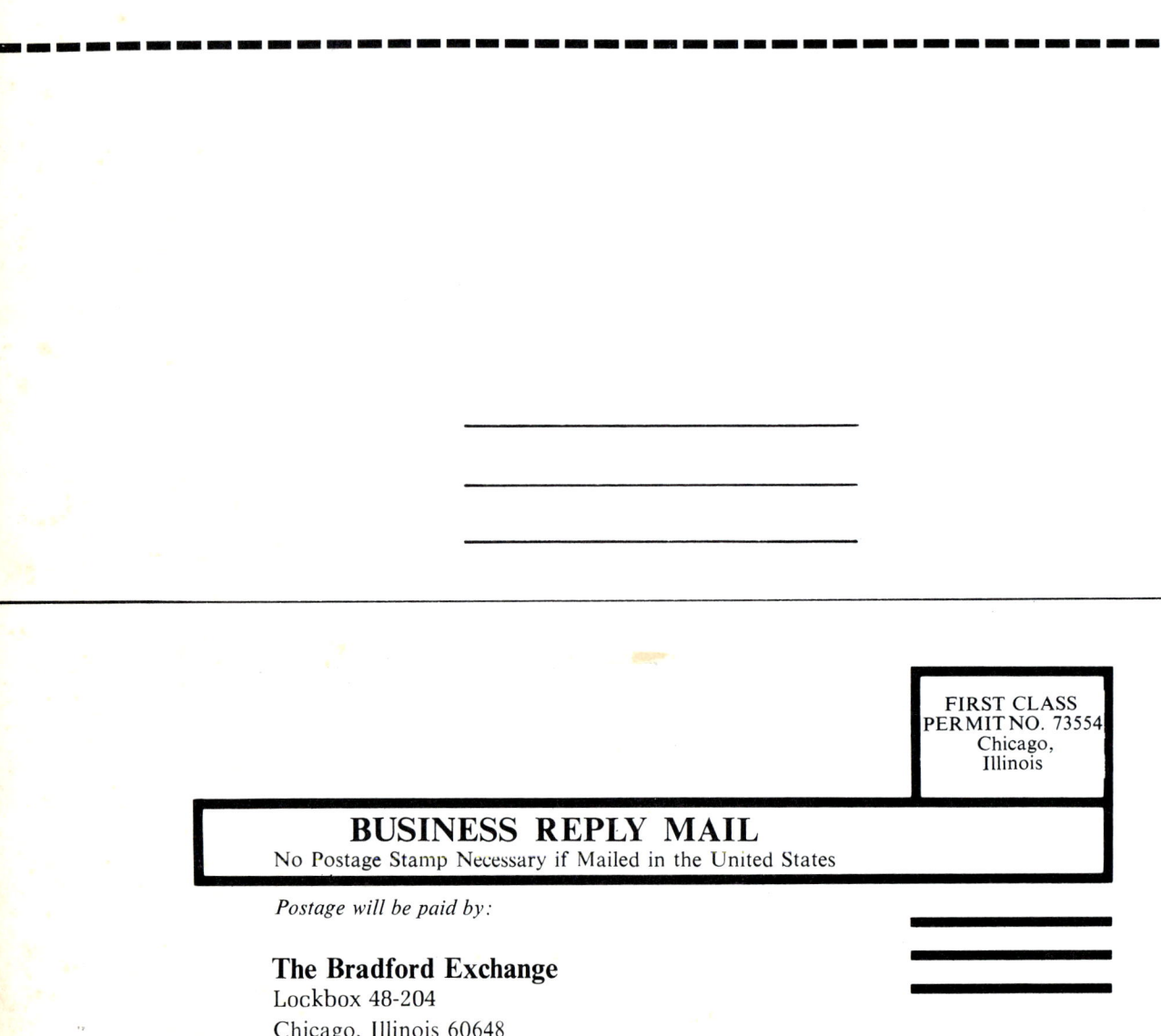

FIRST CLASS
PERMIT NO. 73554
Chicago, Illinois

BUSINESS REPLY MAIL
No Postage Stamp Necessary if Mailed in the United States

Postage will be paid by:

The Bradford Exchange
Lockbox 48-204
Chicago, Illinois 60648

Have you completed your subscription form?